Champions

Other books by Simon & Schuster Ltd
in conjunction with *The Daily Express*

Nigel Mansell: World Champion, The Full Story

Champions

The 26 Year Quest for Glory

The story of Manchester United's winning season

Complied by
FRANK MALLEY

SIMON & SCHUSTER

LONDON · SYDNEY · NEW · YORK · TOKYO · SINGAPORE · TORONTO

First published in Great Britain by Simon & Schuster Ltd, 1993
A Paramount Communications Company
Copyright © Express Newspapers plc, 1993

Simon & Schuster Ltd
West Garden Place
Kendal Street
London W2 2AQ

Simon & Schuster of Australia Pty Ltd
Sydney

A CIP catalogue record for this book is available from the British Library.

ISBN 0–671–85264–7

Typeseting and halftone origination SLG Business Services
Colour Reproduction Keene Engraving
Printed in Great Britain by The Bath Press

Contents

Foreword

At last they've done it! And no-one could have been more delighted than me to see Manchester United win the League title again after 26 years. The memories came flooding back those glorious times in the Sixties when the Beatles ruled the world of music and United were winning everything in sight. We played to packed houses everywhere, we had great players, the atmosphere was fabulous and there were some wonderful goals.

They were great, great days ... the best 13 years of my life. All of us from the 1967 side are Manchester United fans and we've sat back and waited a great length of time to savour that feeling again.

United have had some success, it's true, in Cup competitions but the League Championship was the Holy Grail. The bigger the club the more important it becomes. Now United have done it they could dominate like Liverpool did in the '80s.

In my day we regularly had 20,000 locked out at Old Trafford. It could be repeated with people all over flocking to see the most charismatic team in the country. I was at Crystal Palace a while ago and read one of their old match reports. We had 40,000 there watching one of our games in the 1970's – and I wouldn't bet against it all happening again.

A lot of managers and players since the glory days have been put under pressure by what we achieved and the way we played. I hope that can be put to the back of people's minds now – but I hope they don't forget us altogether. The 1993 title-winning team is the most exciting United side since I played. They don't seem to have a weakness and have three or four players who can turn a game on their own just like we had in Bobby Charlton, Denis Law and myself.

The most important thing from my point of view, though, was that Alex Ferguson built a side with flair. They won it from start to finish with attacking football. I would hate any team to win the League by playing the long ball stuff.

They may have changed their style in previous years but this time they had Cantona. I had my doubts, but he's been an inspired signing and proved Alex Ferguson right.

Ryan Giggs was the jewel in the Championship crown. The most important quality for any great sportsman to possess is balance. Ryan has it all. He can ride tackles, change direction and produce the most audacious body swerves. There are times when I see myself in Ryan's play. We both think our team-mates should give us the ball at every opportunity. If we lose possession we see it as a personal insult. I love watching Ryan snapping at opponents' ankles to get the ball back when he's lost it. I used to feel the same. It's a matter of pride.

Giggs does things for his team that nobody else in the British game can match. Old Trafford was made for players like Ryan to display their talent. I hope we can savour his special ability there for many years to come. A lot of clubs should take notice and start to play the way Manchester United play. I don't see any reason why United shouldn't be THE team again for a large part of the Nineties. Since the heady days of the Sixties when United last ruled football in this country, Nottingham Forest, Liverpool and Arsenal have taken over at various stages, leaving United in the background.

This could be the start of the new United era. I have a great deal of respect for manager Alex Ferguson and the way he has stuck to the toughest job in football. A couple of years ago people were calling for his head, and the chairman's, but they turned the club round.

Ferguson nurtured and brought the best players in the country. He forged a tremendous supply of youth talent and, of course, there was lots of money coming in through the gates.

He could strengthen the team if he wanted to, but I reckon his Championship side could be winning big prizes for years. Yes … the glory days are back at Old Trafford.

George Best

We are the Champions

It was the simplest and yet the most spontaneous of gestures. The brand new solid silver Premier League trophy, designed and manufactured by Garrards, the Queen's jewellers, has a lid in the shape of a crown. For Steve Bruce it was irresistible. He detached it from the trophy and placed it on the head of Bryan Robson.

With that symbolic movement he was indicating that though Robson had been less involved in the lifting of the Championship than a number of other players, he was still their leader and their inspiration.

It was a touching tribute to Robson's own part in the development by Alex Ferguson of a football team worthy of bringing back the game's most prestigious prize to its premier club after a wait of 26 years.

The fact that the issue had been decided while the Manchester United players had been relaxing on Sunday May 2nd was hardly relevant, because the League had really been won over the gruelling months that preceded it.

What Oldham Athletic's 1-0 victory over Aston Villa did was to turn the following day into one of prolonged celebration. What was expected to be the decisive night of the season turned instead into a colourful carnival when Old Trafford, bedecked in red and white, staged one enormous, energetic and engaging party.

There had been champagne taken on Sunday night in the leafy lanes of Cheshire by players who had assembled at each other's homes. The manager's doors had been opened to his friends and neighbours. It was not, it must be admitted, quite the kind of conduct Fergie would normally have condoned from his players, or indeed from himself, on the eve of a big match, but in the circumstances it was understandable.

It was a lovely day for an out-of-doors party with spring in the air. No doubt a brisk morning walk would clear away the fuzzy head and the aftertaste of the Moet and Chandon. Most of the players enjoyed a lie-in, their slumbers undisturbed by any concern about the outcome of the match. No waking in the night this time with the nagging worry that there was still another 90 minutes to be negotiated.

The relief that the result against Blackburn Rovers no longer mattered was not allowed to disturb the professionalism of the United players.

Back at the ground, looking pristine in the pale sunshine of the dawn, the crowds were already gathering. From six o'clock on Sunday evening street vendors had been doing brisk sales in T-shirts celebrating the title win. Some had been there all night, sleeping where the celebrations had ended the previous night beside the street whose name has been changed to Sir Matt Busby Way.

They were descending on Manchester not just from Lancashire but from all parts of the country, for this is the football club which, like Marks and Spencer, seems to have branches everywhere. Actually 128 of them, and all enjoying vigorous membership.

Many travelled this day without hope of seeing the game from inside Old Trafford, for the ground might easily have been filled three times over. Work had gone on apace all season at the Old Stretford End to meet the demands of the Taylor Report for an all-seater stadium. It was partially open, but if there is a sadness about this victory year it is that so many of the younger supporters who have endured season after season of frustration were unable to be there at the finest hour.

Thankfully, in the environs of the ground and around the country wherever there was a satellite dish, Sky Television were

United's Red Army start to party at Old Trafford.

staging an extravaganza of a programme and bringing together a number of the heroes of the 1967 side to add their appreciation of the team that had at last stepped from their very considerable shadow.

If there were tens of thousands of supporters disappointed at not being able to say to their grandchildren "I was there," then at least they had the benefit of glimpses behind the scenes which they could not have enjoyed from a seat in the stand.

As the players gathered at the ground they were left with no doubts about the depth of emotion their success had generated. The queues around the souvenir shop would have done justice to the Harrods Sale, and the bubbling conversations were being conducted in a variety of accents and languages.

The extent of the feelings for Manchester United is never easy to explain, but there is little doubt much of it was generated by the events of February 6, 1958, when the young team Sir Matt Busby built perished in the snow on the runway of Munich Airport. They were remembered too, amid the celebrations, by groups who gathered beneath the Old Trafford clock that never ticks, frozen at 2.30 p.m., the time the aircraft pitched into the freezing earth.

Inside the dressing room the players talked of how they had spent that previous afternoon. Despite instructions to the contrary

The striken Elizabethan aircraft, which claimed the lives of seven United players, lies on the Munich runway.

from their manager some had been watching events at Villa Park, while others had been out visiting friends. The manager had decided he would not endure the game, since he could not influence the outcome.

"Whatever had happened at Villa Park I knew that our destiny was in our own hands," Ferguson said. "When you have the pole position you don't have to concern yourself with what is going on behind you. I decided I would be out of the house and on the golf course with my eldest son."The atmosphere beneath the main stand, was one of relaxed enjoyment of a job well done. It was so different from how it might have been had victory against Blackburn been needed. But at the same time the manager was anxious that his team should show the watching world the quality of the football which had taken them to their own particular Everest. Victory was certainly not essential. But it was desirable.

While the team changed into the football strip millions of youngsters yearn to wear, the atmosphere inside the ground was building.

The late Freddie Mercury's "We Are The Champions" boomed deafeningly from the Old Trafford speakers and tissues were applied to misty eyes.

It was a fitting occasion for Ferguson to be presented with the Barclays Manager Award for the month of April for it was in that final lap of the long-distance race that United had really found their sprint finish. The crowd acclaimed the man who had spent seven seasons at the club in pursuit of the elusive dream. The jeroboam of champagne that went with the salver was not destined to stay long uncorked.

The applause when the team emerged, with Paul Ince, as usual, straggling behind the rest, was deafening. But Blackburn, with six victories in their previous seven matches, were determined to be the party poopers. And when Kevin Gallacher knocked in an eighth-minute goal they appeared to be just that.

The goal turned down the volume momentarily, though the realisation that it wouldn't really matter gave the crowd back their voice. And it reached peak level as Ryan Giggs, the symbol of United's present and future, lifted a soaring free-kick into the roof of the Rovers net. It was, truly, Ryan of the Rovers stuff.

And when, in the second half, their dearly beloved Robbo was introduced it sent the fans into delirium. There was no way now that this game could end in anything other than a United victory, and Eric Cantona, chic and stylish and so much an influence on United this season, duly supplied the ammunition for Ince to fire United into the lead. Now was the time to introduce Andrei Kanchelskis, United's express from the Ukraine. How far from the austerity of Eastern Europe Old Trafford must have seemed to him that night.

The script was completed in the very last minutes of the game when United won the free-kick that enabled Gary Pallister to step forward and score his first goal of this momentous season and become the last outfield player in the side to claim a goal.

Yet the goal that had really won the title had come the previous day, and from a player who had been brought up to regard Manchester United as the enemy on the doorstep. His name was Nick Henry, and he plied his trade for Oldham Athletic, the side that operated in the shadow of United and Manchester City. Henry is a Liverpudlian, from the city which in the sporting sense attempts to pretend that Manchester doesn't exist. And, in football terms, it hasn't over the last 25 years.

Oldham had gone to Birmingham on that Sunday night in desperate need of points in their battle to avoid relegation. But Villa knew also that if they were to re-kindle the embers of their own challenge on United, they too, had to collect the maximum three points.

Villa, clearly, were the favourites to win this match with ease and so apply the pressure on United. Their best expectation was to beat Oldham, for Blackburn to defeat United and for the issue to be decided on the last day of the season when both travelled to London, Villa at QPR and United at Wimbledon.

There was some irony in the situation, for Villa manager Ron Atkinson had been a popular manager of Manchester United, one of five bosses between Sir Matt and Fergie who had tried and failed to find the Holy Grail. He wrote in his programme notes for the game: "The title is still there to be won." And on the face of it, so it was.

But Villa's nerve had gone. They had travelled to Blackburn eight days earlier and lost heavily, and it had inflicted on their morale a lasting scar. And while Ferguson was following his drive down the 10th hole at Mottram Hall Golf and Country Club, young Nick Henry was bringing the 1992-93 inaugural Premier League season to a premature climax.

It was not, perhaps, the most spectacular goal of this invigorating season. But it was certainly the most crucial. It started with a throw-in on the left side of midfield to Neil Pointon, a full-back who himself had played in United's shadow at Maine Road for two seasons before moving to Boundary Park.

He looked up, spotted Norwegian international Gunnar Halle

making a break through the inside right position, and delivered a long, cross-field pass. Villa were short of numbers at the back to cope with this counter, and Steve Staunton, late of Liverpool, was the player to contest Pointon's ball.

Halle got there and his header square fell to Manchester-born Darren Beckford. He made a clumsy attempt at control and managed only to help the ball on to where Henry, now in full stride, delivered his angled shot across the body of Villa keeper Mark Bosnich and inside the far post. Dean Saunders was to hit the angle of crossbar and upright four minutes later from a superbly struck free-kick, but that was the nearest they came to an equaliser.

Back at Mottram Hall, Ferguson was stepping onto the 17th tee when a complete stranger strolled up to him and broke the news that United were champions. The celebrations could begin, but first Fergie, the most earnest of competitors, made sure he defeated his son Mark, by a shot before the pop of the first champagne cork was heard.

What that Henry goal had done was to bring to an end a pursuit that had lasted 26 years, which had cost £32m and had embraced five managers. Quite why it had taken so long has been the subject of many debates long into the night with no satisfactory explanation.

The team of '67 consisted of very special and extraordinary talents. It had been a product of the times, for this was the Swinging Sixties of flower power and the Beatles. And United had a Beatle of

BUBBLING ALONG ...
Alex ferguson celebrates in
traditional style.

Dennis Law

their own, whose sublime, awesome talent was not to be matched by any British player then or since. Wherever polls on the great players are held these names always appear on the ballot sheet: Di Stefano, Pele, Cruyff … George Best.

Best embodied the mood of the times and played in a football team whose own expression was indicative of the freedom of the period. They were the symbol of the Sixties, of style with strength. And in addition to Best they had Bobby Charlton and Denis Law to provide a trio of world-class players. All three were at Old Trafford on May 3rd, 1993, to see their ghost finally laid and in many ways grateful that it had been. Others of that class of '67 were also there, David Sadler, Bill Foulkes, Pat Crerand and Nobby Stiles. They know more than most that as the years have rolled along their names have become a millstone to the succession of players who followed them.

Crerand is one of that elite who has remained so close to the club that he can now be identified as a true barometer of terrace opinion, happy to be counted as one of the forever faithful. He was amused on celebration night that among the veritable army who flew from Dublin to Manchester there were a select few who had on the back of their matching sweatshirts "We All Know Paddy Crerand." Who, among United fans, doesn't? He believes it was to the club's pro-longed advantage that the ghosts have been exorcised. What's more, he was generous in his appraisal of the strengths of the new champions, as were most of the class of '67.

"It is important for the club that they have at last won the title. But it is just as important for English football," said the old craftsman, who matched his own artistry with a fearsome steel which Bryan Robson, in particular, of the present generation would have admired. "What is much more pleasing is that they have within them the ability and the quality to win it over again and you know that Alex Ferguson will not be satisfied with what he has got. he will try to entice the best players to the club. I don't care much for the comparisons between the two teams because the game now is so much quicker, so much more intense, and if they want to be creative, players have to think quicker. But what I have seen in this side is what I most admire in a football team, a bit of style matched with a hint of arrogance. That gives the game its beauty. But the place has been alive all this season much more than it was last. I have felt that the good old days were beckoning ever since Eric Cantona walked through the door."

It was not so much what the Frenchman achieved as an individual, which will be traced elsewhere in this appreciation, so much

Bobby Charlton in 1966.

as the way his game affected other people. Crerand, for one, was impressed. "He is infectious. The things he tries to do the others try, and it was the way the team played that had the middle-aged spectators leaping around like infants. A lot of that had to do with the introduction of the Frenchman." Cantona was just one of the potential match-winners who were recognised by their former peers, and it was George Best who suggested that with three or four such players able to turn a game in their own right, the title side could endure for several seasons.

The man who brought them all together with their various talents and temperaments was Alex Ferguson, whose place among the mystical names of Manchester United is now assured, a man whose own background is so identifiable with so many of the working class who form the pillar of United's support. There is a joke road sign adorning his office at The Cliff, the laboratory where experiments with United sides have been conducted over the seasons. It says "Ahcumfigovin" - "I come from Govan" - and is Fergie's own reminder of the Glasgow suburb where he was strictly raised to know right from wrong and where he was urged into an

Busby referees a practice match before the European Cup Final with (left to right) Bobby Charlton and George Best.

engineering apprenticeship and trade union officialdom which helped to give him a sharper appreciation of the rewards of the game.

Ferguson was well acquainted with the enormity of the job he inherited from Ron Atkinson after turning down the manager's chair at Rangers, Arsenal and Tottenham. He had seen the casualty list of managers who had sought and failed to restore to United the glories that Matt Busby had brought them. He had won ten trophies in eight years at Pittodrie, smashed the Glasgow strangle-hold and made himself perhaps the most coveted manager in Britain. Even in his Grampian outpost he knew the names of the men who had tried and failed. First Wilf McGuiness, the young Busby apprentice who had a harrowing 18 months from June 1969 to December 1970 trying to act as His Master's Voice. At the age of 31 he was probably too young and inexperienced to handle the side Matt passed down to him, with Best now a rebellious maverick, as unpredictable as he could be brilliant. It was an experiment which Liverpool had found so successful, of trying to create your own Dynasty. However, after that short, pressurised spell in which he bought only Ian Ure from Arsenal, McGuiness was replaced. He was there, too on celebration night, savouring the occasion as vigorously as the youngest supporters.

When Wilf abdicated to make way for the urbane Irishman Frank O'Farrell, a man more in the Busby mould, there were raised eyebrows in the football ranks and perhaps with just cause. For Frank (June 1971 to December 1972) did not have the charisma

Manager Wilf McGuiness (left) with new signing Ian Ure, chief coach Jimmy Murphy and Matt Busby in 1969.

required to identify with the club's public, who need to enjoy some kind of rapport with the man in charge of the team. They need the feeling that running the club is a shared responsibility. Yet United had O'Farrell to thank for one of the most successful purchases in the quarter century of chasing elusive shadows. He brought Martin Buchan down from Aberdeen, a defender who would be at the heart of United's FA Cup campaigning, leading them into three Wembley finals. Other signings like Wyn Davies, the big Welsh centre-forward, and Ted MacDougall, were less successful. When O'Farrell left the club there was some acrimony because he felt he had not been given sufficient time to develop a side on which he spent £635,000 to bring in five players.

TIGHT-LIPPED …
Manager Frank O'Farrell
moving in at Old Trafford in
July 1971.

There was no doubt, however, about the impact Tommy Docherty made as he breezed into the club just before Christmas 1972, from having managed the Scotland national side. The Doc was to stay with the club for four and a half turbulent years during which they were never far from the headlines. That included the unthinkable in season 1973-74 – relegation to the Second Division, for his first time in 37 years. That, as it transpired, might not have been a bad thing for the club. It enabled them to re-evaluate their playing strategy, to shed some of the fear that was inhibiting their football. Perhaps just as important, the public stayed loyal, as an average gate of 48,388 for the 1974-75 season testified.

The Doc was always active in the transfer market. It was in this period that players like Big Jim Holton, Stroller George Graham, Stewart Houston, later Graham's No 2 at Arsenal, Lou Macari and Gerry Daly were imported, and they not so much worked their way back to the First Division as rocket-propelled themselves there. The First Division needed a healthy Manchester United. And they got one, because for much of the 1975-76 season they ran for the League and FA Cup double. As it was they finished third in the League and reached Wembley, losing the final to Lawrie McMenemy's Southampton. But what United now had was a team more in keeping with their traditions. The Doc had lured two wingers to the club, the cheeky Gordon Hill on the left and the educated and thoughtful Steve Coppell on the right.

United were back at Wembley the following season, and this time they defeated treble-chasing Liverpool with goals from two more of the free-spending Doc's purchases, Stuart "Pancho" Pearson and Jimmy Greenhoff. The Doc, it seemed, had found the remedy. He was ebullient and full of bravado. But dismissal was only two months away. "After becoming a cardinal in this cathedral

Tommy Docherty

who could go back to being a parish priest," was his famous boast. But he was to face excommunication after he admitted falling in love in love with the club physiotherapist's wife, Mary Brown. The Doc departed with his ambition unfulfilled, but having looked the most likely of the incumbents since Sir Matt to break the now worrying absence of League success.

Neither did it come either under Dave Sexton, who took over in August 1977. Here was a manager so utterly different in style and temperament from the tempestuous Docherty, a respected coach who found media relations difficult but who in friendship had a lovely waspish sense of humour.

Sexton also brought excellent players to Old Trafford, Joe Jordan and Gordon McQueen from Leeds, Kevin Moran from Ireland and Ray Wilkins from Chelsea. Indeed, he spent more than £3.5m on 10 players in his three and a half years. But again his labours were not destined to produce a title-winning side, though again they reached the FA Cup final, in 1979, and were beaten 3-2, this time in a nail-biter with Arsenal.

By April 1981 it was again time for change, as the worry over winning the Championship veered towards crisis. Now there was no scramble among managers for a job that clearly had pressures some were not prepared to shoulder, or at least to leave secure and comfortable jobs for. Ron Atkinson knew that he was well down the Board's list of contenders. But he didn't hesitate

Dave Sexton on his way into Manchester.

to accept the post, believing he had not only the personality and charisma for it, but the ability too. This was, without doubt, an era of some success for the club. Atkinson was not only an immensely popular figure on the Manchester sporting scene, he was unlucky not to have broken the stranglehold of the team from his native city, Liverpool. For five flamboyant years Atkinson moulded his sides around Bryan Robson, whom he took to the club for £1.5m from West Brom. In total Atkinson spent in excess of £7.5m but in return the club was always threatening Liverpool's domination without quite being able to break it. His sides never finished outside the top four in the First Division and there were three visits to Wembley. But still the dream eluded him. Atkinson was unlucky not to be given at least one extra season, but perhaps what finally drove

Ron Atkinson … on the run.

chairman Martin Edwards to replace him was a spate of transfers in 1985 and '86 which did not prove fruitful – players like Peter Barnes, Colin Gibson, Terry Gibson and Peter Davenport. The chairman's eyes were now directed at the Granite City. Alex Ferguson had conclusively broken the grip of Glasgow clubs and was ready for a new challenge.

Ferguson now reflects that no manager can ever really be prepared for the task of managing Manchester United. There is no suitable apprenticeship and Fergie believes he spent his first four seasons coming to terms with the pressures and the politics. It was the first time he had encountered a club where the sheer volume of support commanded respect from the manager. Not only did they demand victory, they wanted it with flair, style and boldness. But he found it was a drug and he became as involved in their desire for success as it was possible to be, the manager, yet a fan of the club. The need to entertain at all costs became obsessive. Ferguson knew from his days as a fan on the Ibrox territory that the week could revolve around those 90 minutes.

Alex Ferguson points the way.

His first three forays into the transfer market brought Brian McClair, Viv Anderson and Steve Bruce to Manchester. Indeed, there were to be few questionable purchases in those first three years. Buys included Mark Hughes, Lee Sharpe, Gary Pallister and Paul Ince. Some failed, of course, like Ralph Milne and, to a lesser extent, Danny Wallace.

But while he was rebuilding his senior squad Ferguson was also overhauling the youth set-up at Old Trafford, which he had found lacked organisation and a systematic control. Concurrent with building a Championship side he invested the club with some of the best young talent in the country, no mean achievement. Yet it wasn't an easy ride in those early seasons, and after he was appointed in November 1986, United finished in a very ordinary mid-table position. His second season was much better with United finishing runners-up to Liverpool but still nine points behind them. This was the year too when he had to deal with indiscipline in the ranks which put him on a collision course with two of the crowd's favourites, Norman Whiteside and Paul McGrath. Both, he decided, had to go.

In 1988-89 it was Arsenal's turn to contest the title with Liverpool and United were languishing a disappointing 13th as the issue was decided in a thrilling final match at Anfield. It was the season when Ferguson agonised over Gordon Strachan's sale to Leeds, but brought in Neil Webb and Pallister as the re-structuring went on. But would he be given the time to continue that painstaking business of finding the winning formula? There is little doubt that as football moved into the Nineties Ferguson was in danger of becoming just another statistic in the stockpile of failed managers. The knives were out for him because a summer investment of £7m in the market place still did not produce the results. What saved him was the FA Cup. Yet as the pressure built on him from outside, behind the closed doors of the ground support was forthcoming from chairman Martin Edwards. He remembered what Sir Matt had told him and stopped buying the papers.

United finished eighth from bottom of the First Division, but two superb FA Cup semi-finals against Oldham Athletic and a winning final replay against Crystal Palace bought Ferguson the valuable extra time he needed. It was the season when the fans were given their first fleeting glimpse of Ryan Giggs and Andrei Kanchelskis. But, above all, it was the season of a notable European Cup Winners' Cup success with the memorable final victory against Johan Cruyff's Barcelona in Rotterdam. It was the season when the fans adopted "Always Look On The Bright Side Of Life" from the film

The Life of Brian. It somehow summed up the philosophy of those who worship at the United shrine. United had been persecuted now for almost 25 years for failing to regain the League title.

But the signs were there now, and in 1991-92 they seemed to have the title within their grasp, only to lose out in the last few matches of the season to Leeds United, a defeat which affected Ferguson deeply during the summer. "I knew we had thrown it away but what hurt me so much was the satisfaction our rivals seemed to take from the team's demise. I found it difficult to understand."

The gloating only increased the determination to atone for the bitter disappointment. "Some setbacks don't just numb you, they smack you right between the eyes and leave a vacuum in your life, a void that just seems inescapable," Ferguson said. He retreated to Sweden with his wife and stayed in the countryside outside Gothenberg attending the European Championship as part of his rehabilitation. Ferguson is a man of immense inner strength and determination and now he was not going to wallow in self-pity. He felt he owed it to the enduringly loyal supporters to launch a more searching challenge to regain the mantle of the very best club in the country.

"Two or three seasons ago I said I wanted to build a team that could mount a few challenges and which was young enough to accept those challenges. They have proven that and we want to develop a competitive edge that will not endure for one season but for some time to come," said Ferguson. He came home from Sweden determined that United would strive to be the champions in the inaugural Premier League season. And maybe as he glanced at the FA Charity Shield match and noticed that Eric Cantona had scored a hat trick for Leeds United something in his subconscious was stirring.

Match Reports

15 August to 21 November

*How Cantona came
saw and conquered*

28 November to 9 May

Hughes, chased by Giggs, salutes his goal against Forest.

August 15

SHEFFIELD UNITED 2

MANCHESTER UNITED 1

(Half-time score: 1-0)

Sheff Utd: Tracey, Gage, McLeary, Beesley, Barnes, Bradshaw, Lake, Gannon (Hartfield 87), Hodges (Bryson 68), Cork, Deane. Sub: Kelly
Scorer: Deane 5, 50 (pen)
Booked: Gannon, Lake
Man Utd: Schmeichel, Irwin, Blackmore, Bruce, Ferguson, Pallister, Kanchelskis (Dublin 68), Ince (Phelan 7), McClair, Hughes, Giggs. Sub: Walsh
Scorer: Hughes 62
Booked: Blackmore
Referee: B Hill (Kettering)
Attendance: 28,070
Weather: Fine

OH NO! … Alex Ferguson shows his despair as United's season starts with a 2–1 defeat at Bramall Lane.

The new season was barely five minutes old and Manchester United had already conceded the first goal in Premier League history. As Brian Deane's header flew past goalkeeper Peter Schmeichel, championship glory was nine months and a million miles away.

Sheffield United's fans were delighted. It was really true … the Red Devils were a spent force. Self-doubt ran through this first performance of the new campaign. United's lack of confidence too often left them a yard short as anticipation gave way to hesitation.

They were still good players – few would argue about that. But their spirit was definitely questionable. Perhaps there really was a jinx on United's title aspirations. Perhaps luck would always manage to give them a kick in the teeth no matter how well they played.

Sheffield's second goal after 50 minutes was the perfect illustration. Veteran Alan Cork, hardly the speediest of forwards, bustled onto a through pass from Deane and went crashing over as United's England international centre-back Gary Pallister moved in to challenge. Referee Brian Hill awarded the penalty and Deane tucked away the spot-kick to the fury of the United supporters banked behind Schmeichel's goal.

United's troubles could have been worse. If not for Schmeichel's prompt action in intercepting an angry Manchester fan heading for referee Hill defeat may have been followed by an FA inquiry. But with United's 6ft 3in goalkeeper staring down at him the invader did not stand much chance of reaching his target.

Kettering official Hill said afterwards: "I didn't see the fan but Peter probably did me a big favour."

Fergie had some sympathy for the irate supporter, accusing Mr Hill of having a stinker. "We don't want this man to referee our games again," he said. "It was a tragedy for us to see a supporter run on in that manner. I've not seen that from a United fan before. Goodness knows what might have happened if Schmeichel hadn't intervened"

Schmeichel said: "I though Gary got the ball first. The ref made a bad decision but if the fan got on the pitch there might have been another 10 after him."

But it was the penalty that got away that really angered Ferguson. Even the Sheffield players looked on in disbelief when goalkeeper Simon Tracey's dive across Ryan Giggs in the 19th minute was not penalised. Ferguson's demand that Hill be kept clear of United in future was not a spur-of-the-moment protest. It was fuelled by bad memories of the official in previous matches against Wimbledon and Forest.

A rash challenge by midfielder Paul Ince on Tracey added to Fergie's worries. Ince suffered a hip injury which threatened to rule him out of the approaching midweek match with Everton at Old Trafford.

In truth, there was little satisfaction for United apart from a late goal by Mark Hughes, pairing up for the first time with £1 million substitute Dion Dublin for the last 20 minutes.

But it was clear that Ferguson was not going to allow his players to use the excuse that they were still suffering from last season's title hangover much longer. Alan Cork explained: "I might have ruined a few careers the way I went past their defenders at my pace. Their manager was in the dressing room giving them a right going over."

League Table After Match

	P	W	D	L	F	A	Pts
Norwich	1	1	0	0	4	2	3
Coventry	1	1	0	0	2	1	3
Leeds	1	1	0	0	2	1	3
Sheff Utd	1	1	0	0	2	1	3
Blackburn	1	0	1	0	3	3	1
C. Palace	1	0	1	0	3	3	1
Aston Villa	1	0	1	0	1	1	1
Chelsea	1	0	1	0	1	1	1
Everton	1	0	1	0	1	1	1
Ipswich	1	0	1	0	1	1	1
Oldham	1	0	1	0	1	1	1
Sheff Wed	1	0	1	0	1	1	1
Southampton	1	0	1	0	0	0	1
Tottenham	1	0	1	0	0	0	1
Man Utd	1	0	0	1	1	2	0
Middlesbrough	1	0	0	1	1	2	0
Wimbledon	1	0	0	1	1	2	0
Arsenal	1	0	0	1	2	4	0
Liverpool	0	0	0	0	0	0	0
Man City	0	0	0	0	0	0	0
Nottm Forest	0	0	0	0	0	0	0
QPR	0	0	0	0	0	0	0

MANCHESTER UNITED 0

EVERTON 3

(Half-time score: 0-1)

United: Schmeichel, Irwin, Blackmore, Bruce, Ferguson, Pallister, Kanchelskis, Ince (Phelan 45), McClair, Hughes, Giggs (Dublin 82). Sub: Walsh
Booked: Ferguson
Everton: Southall, Harper, Watson, Ablett, Hinchcliffe, Warzycha (Johnston 81), Horne, Ebbrell, Ward, Beardsley, Rideout (Beagrie 72). Sub: Kearton
Scorers: Beardsley 45, Warzycha 81, Johnston 90
Referee: K Barratt (Coventry)
Attendance: 31,901
Weather: Warm

United's first home game in the Premier League produced possibly the strangest result of the season.

The demolition of the Stretford End earlier in the summer did more than remove old steel and concrete. At first the soul seemed to have been torn from the stadium.

In the glory years of the mid-sixties United legend Bobby Charlton used to say he could feel the pull of the Stretford End as a physical force – almost an animal magnet that would draw the ball inexorably into the net.

Now the gaping hole at the west end of the ground gave the stadium an unreal atmosphere, as if the supporters who used to roar on their team from the old terracing had been muted by their transfer to a seat in the stands.

But if the aura was unreal so was the humiliating scoreline. United had not played that badly yet they had been crushed by a goal just before half-time and two in the last 10 minutes. Now with two matches gone, the pre-season hot favourites for the title were sitting forlornly at the bottom of the table.

Everton's Peter Beardsley was the demolition expert who placed the charges under United. Beardsley, once rejected by Ron Atkinson

AIR FORCE …
Everton goalkeeper Neville
Southall defies United.

after a brief trial period at Old Trafford, had gone on to win England stardom and a cabinet full of medals with Newcastle and Liverpool … but he always seemed delighted to put one over on the club who did not want him.

Beardsley gave Everton the lead shortly before the interval, running onto a pass from Polish ace Robert Warzycha before wrong-footing goalkeeper Peter Schmeichel and steering the ball into the empty net.

In the 80th minute Beardsley returned the favour, feeding Warzycha, who left centre-half Gary Pallister for dead before smashing his drive high into the corner of the net.

Mo Johnston's third goal, with the last kick of the match, was no more than putting the boot into an opponent already on his knees and beaten into submission.

But United manager Alex Ferguson seemed more angered than alarmed by his team's sorry start. He said: "You sometimes need an embarrassing sickener like that to jolt you into action.

"But to win things you need discipline and defensively we lacked it and were punished.

"We have to go back to the basics. Some of our football was very good in the first half-hour and it is a strange game when you see a scoreline like that one."

It is true United created many chances but Everton goalkeeper Neville Southall was in the kind of form that once saw him hailed as the best in the world. Certainly his Welsh international team-mate Mark Hughes was in no mood to argue after seeing Southall stop everything he could throw at him.

Southall also saved superbly from teenage prodigy Ryan Giggs before United were rocked back on their heels by Beardsley's goal.

That blow, and the half-time loss of Paul Ince who was clearly still struggling with the injury he suffered at Bramall Lane, left United looking curiously disjointed.

In contrast to the brilliant Southall, United's Schmeichel looked an uncertain pretender to the crown as the world's No 1 goalkeeper. Clearly unsure as to the ramifications of the season's new backpass law, Schmeichel chested down a long ball from Everton's Gary Ablett only to see it bounce clear for Johnston to score in injury time.

One man who saw nothing strange in the scoreline was Everton manager Howard Kendall. Looking forward with some optimism he said: "I don't feel this was an astonishing result because we are capable of producing scorelines like that against anyone. This will give us belief in ourselves."

Danger–man Beardsley is closely marked by Clayton Blackmore.

League Table After Match

	P	W	D	L	F	A	Pts
Norwich	2	2	0	0	6	3	6
Coventry	2	2	0	0	4	1	6
Everton	2	1	1	0	4	1	4
QPR	2	1	1	0	4	2	4
Sheff Wed.	2	1	1	0	3	1	4
Blackburn	2	1	1	0	4	3	4
Leeds	2	1	1	0	3	2	4
Ipswich	2	1	1	0	2	1	4
Middlesbrough	2	1	0	1	3	2	3
Sheff Utd	2	1	0	1	3	3	3
Liverpool	2	1	0	1	2	2	3
Nottm Forest	2	1	0	1	1	2	3
C. Palace	2	0	2	0	4	4	2
Aston Villa	2	0	2	0	2	2	2
Oldham	2	0	2	0	2	2	2
Chelsea	2	0	1	1	2	3	1
Man City	2	0	1	1	2	3	1
Southampton	2	0	1	1	1	3	1
Tottenham	2	0	1	1	0	2	1
Wimbledon	2	0	0	2	1	3	0
Arsenal	2	0	0	2	2	5	0
MAN UTD	2	0	0	2	1	5	0

August 22

MANCHESTER UNITED 1

IPSWICH 1

(Half-time score: 0-0)

United: Schmeichel, Irwin, Blackmore (Webb 66), Bruce, Ferguson, Pallister, Kanchelskis (Dublin 86), Phelan, McClair, Hughes, Giggs. Sub: Walsh
Scorer: Irwin 57
Ipswich: Forrest, Stockwell, Wark, Linighan, Whelan (Milton 83), Dozzell (Youds 74), Williams, Thompson, Kiwomya, Goddard, Johnson. Sub: Baker
Scorer: Kiwomya 56
Booked: Wark, Whelan
Referee: G Ashby (Worcester)
Attendance: 31,704
Weather: Wet

United's faithful were growing restless. Three matches into the season their team had picked up just one point and scored only two goals. What the hell was going on?

Words of comfort came from an unexpected source. Ipswich veteran John Wark had seen it all. Now 37, Wark had collected a bagful of medals as an attacking midfielder with Ipswich and Liverpool as well as playing World Cup football with Scotland.

These days Wark was back in Suffolk, the old hand at the heart of Ipswich defence, and played a key role in shackling Mark Hughes and Brian McClair in front of 31,000 Old Trafford fans.

But afterwards the craggy Scot insisted United had no need to panic. Wark observed: "There's not much wrong with United. I fancy them to finish in the top three – even win it!"

Few paid any attention to Wark's words at the time. Tommy Docherty, an ex-United manager working on local radio, was particularly harsh in his Press criticism of Gary Pallister.

The Doc said Pallister was having a nightmare start to the season and accused him of taking too many chances on the ball.

United's players immediately refused further interviews with Piccadilly Radio, for which Docherty was the regular soccer commentator, and manager Alex Ferguson was quick to defend Pallister.

Ferguson said: "There are a few people having a go at Gary and he won't ignore the criticism because it does hurt.

"Gary can only answer the criticism by performing in the style we've grown accustomed to in recent seasons.

"That's his only way out now. He's worked so hard this summer after missing the European Championships with England and I'm sure it will pay off." Against Ipswich United's best chance of making the breakthrough appeared to be on the flanks but when Ryan Giggs twice took off on penetrating runs into the Ipswich half he ran headlong into Wark like a train hitting the buffers.

In the end it was Ipswich who took the lead after another untidy piece of defending. Jason Dozzell got a touch and Chris Kiwomya squeezed the ball past Peter Schmeichel from close range.

United skipper Steve Bruce said: "The lad was a bit lucky. It hit him on the chest as he ran in and fell nicely for him."

United's equaliser came from Denis Irwin. He blasted away the gloom with an eye-popping 25-yard blast, the first of several vital goals he was to contribute over a long, hard season.

With Ince still out injured manager's son Darren Ferguson, at 20, tried hard to do a man's job in United's midfield until Neil Webb arrived 24 minutes from time to take on the workload.

Substitute Dion Dublin had even less time to make an impression – just four minutes. Dublin, at 6ft 3ins the tallest striker in United's history, had been given just 36 minutes action in three games. But with Alex Ferguson desperate to galvanise his team's fortunes the shaven-headed attacker was about to be handed his big chance.

NUMBER ONE …
Denis Irwin celebrates his first goal of the season.

League Table After Match

	P	W	D	L	F	A	Pts
Coventry	3	3	0	0	6	2	9
Norwich	3	2	1	0	7	4	7
QPR	3	2	1	0	7	4	7
Blackburn	3	2	1	0	5	3	7
Middlesbrough	3	2	0	1	7	3	6
Everton	3	1	2	0	5	2	5
Oldham	3	1	2	0	7	5	5
Sheff Wed.	3	1	2	0	6	4	5
Ipswich	3	1	2	0	3	2	5
Leeds	3	1	1	1	4	6	4
C. Palace	3	0	3	0	6	6	3
Aston Villa	3	0	3	0	3	3	3
Liverpool	2	1	0	1	2	2	3
Sheff Utd	3	1	0	2	5	6	3
Nottm Forest	3	1	0	2	4	7	3
Chelsea	3	0	2	1	5	6	2
Tottenham	3	0	2	1	2	4	2
Southampton	4	0	2	2	2	5	2
Man City	3	0	1	2	1	4	1
MAN UTD	4	0	1	2	2	6	1
Arsenal	2	0	0	2	2	5	0
Wimbledon	3	0	0	3	2	5	0

August 24

Dion Dublin provided Manchester United with a last-minute winner just as concern was developing into alarm.

Dublin, a £1 million signing from Cambridge, might have been very much second choice behind Alan Shearer on Manchester United's wanted list but as he sidefooted the winner with the seconds ticking away Alex Ferguson would not have swapped him for the Crown Jewels.

"He gives us an alternative United have not had for many years," said a delighted Ferguson. "He did very well. Apart from scoring his first goal for us he linked in well with the rest of the side. Joe Jordan was the last United striker like that."

Dublin, in his first full match for United, allied his muscular strength with some deft touches throughout a wind and rain-lashed night. But until the dying seconds there had been no suggestion of what United really needed – a player with that most saleable of commodities, a devastating finish.

So when Mark Hughes headed down Darren Ferguson's free-kick and Dublin tucked it away you could almost hear the gasp of relief from United's bench. Dublin said: "I was not thinking about the time on the clock when the ball came over. I just thought if I can hit it I will get my first goal of the season. Luckily, that's what I did.

"This goal will help me settle down and relax a little more. I was nervous before the match but the £1 million tag did not bother me. It is just a question of ability, nothing else, and the fans will help me to settle in after this. We deserved to win but in the end we got a little bit of luck."

Indeed, it was no more than United deserved for it was they who played most of the real football in this live TV match. Southampton had been swinging the revolving door all summer with players coming in and going out, but not even the reunion of Kerry Dixon and David Speedie, the partnership once so productive at Chelsea, could lift the gloom.

Southampton's long-ball game, with the midfield players simply trying to pick up loose ends, is tedious and unattractive.

It contrasted sharply with United's more fluent approach which was let down only by a wayward final ball and poor finishing.

Ryan Giggs had sifted through his entire repertoire of silky skills to kick-start his side, but each time he tried the starter motor the fuel tank was dry. Even so, there was every suggestion that this victory might give United the injection they so desperately needed.

They could have been in trouble early on when Peter Schmeichel scooped up a Francis Benali free-kick from Dixon's toe. After that it was United who carved all the openings with the driving Paul Ince once again their motivator. He created the chance for Hughes to put Brian McClair in a goal-scoring position which Tim Flowers denied with a most courageous save.

Flowers was penalised by referee Ray Lewis for falling on what was adjudged to be a back-pass from Ken Monkou at the edge of the six-yard box. The rule, introduced in a bid to eliminate time-wasting, only caused more as Lewis tried to keep the Saints wall on their goal-line.

When Flowers sprang forward before the free-kick was taken he became the eighth Southampton player to be cautioned in four matches.

United continued to be wasteful and almost paid for it when Dixon hammered a shot just over the crossbar. Dublin, in fact, missed a chance in the 57th minute and looked like fluffing his lines after taking centre stage. But he was word perfect for his big scene just before the final curtain and his audience of United fans in the 15,623 crowd gave him a standing ovation.

David Speedie chases Paul Ince.

League Table After Match

	P	W	D	L	F	A	Pts
Coventry	3	3	0	0	6	2	9
Norwich	3	2	1	0	7	4	7
QPR	3	2	1	0	7	4	7
Blackburn	3	2	1	0	5	3	7
Middlesbrough	3	2	0	1	7	3	6
Everton	3	1	2	0	5	2	5
Oldham	3	1	2	0	7	5	5
Sheff Wed	3	1	2	0	6	4	5
Ipswich	3	1	2	0	3	2	5
Leeds	3	1	1	1	4	6	4
MAN UTD	4	1	1	2	3	6	4
C. Palace	3	0	3	0	6	6	3
Aston Villa	3	0	3	0	3	3	3
Sheff Utd	3	1	0	2	5	6	3
Arsenal	3	1	0	2	4	5	3
Liverpool	3	1	0	2	2	4	3
Nottm Forest	3	1	0	2	4	7	3
Chelsea	3	0	2	1	5	6	2
Tottenham	3	0	2	1	2	4	2
Southampton	4	0	2	2	5	2	2
Man City	3	0	1	2	1	4	1
Wimbledon	3	0	0	3	2	5	0

August 29

NOTTINGHAM FOREST 0

MANCHESTER UNITED 2

(Half-time score: 0-0)

Forest: Crossley, Laws, Wilson, Chettle, Pearce, Crosby, Keane, Gemmill, Woan, Bannister, Clough. Subs: Orlygsson, Black, Marriott
United: Schmeichel, Phelan (Blackmore 44), Irwin, Bruce, Ferguson, Pallister, Dublin, Ince, McClair, Hughes (Kanchelskis 86), Giggs. Sub: Walsh
Scorers: Hughes 16, Giggs 50
Booked: Dublin, Bruce
Referee: K Redfearn (Whitely Bay)
Attendance: 19,694
Weather: Showers

BATTLE STATIONS …
Dion Dublin gets to grips with Forest's Stuart Pearce as Scott Gemmill (right) looks on.

Mark Hughes set United on the way to their second win in successive away matches but he still wasn't satisfied. Sparky, who later suffered an ankle injury, drove home through a tangle of Forest legs after 15 minutes but said later: "It was a nice strike but as a team we're still not up to the standard of last year. We're not yet steamrolling teams like we did then but two away wins in a row has boosted us all."

Although Ryan Giggs sealed victory just after half-time with a deft header, the teething problems United experienced in linking Hughes with Dion Dublin in a new-look attack formation were sometimes painfully obvious. Their similarity in style saw them collide more than once as both instinctively took up the same position in United's forward thrusts.

But Alex Ferguson stressed the positive aspect of Dublin's contribution, praising his efforts in curtailing forward runs by Forest skipper Stuart Pearce. Fergie said: "We detailed one of our forwards to mark Pearce when we lost possession to stop his runs. Dion worked very hard at that and this was a great result for us.

"He was also well involved in our approach play. Dion showed he has good control of the ball, although we knew that when we bought him from Cambridge."

It was ironic that Pearce was given such a hard time the day he was being widely tipped as the new England captain. His international ambitions seemed about to be fulfilled but his Forest career was in turmoil. Manager Brian Clough had very publicly turned down Pearce's request for a pay rise, prompting speculation that his days at the City Ground were numbered.

United were among a host of clubs, including Liverpool and Inter Milan, expected to fight for Pearce's signature should he become available. But the most worrying factor for Pearce was his form, which so far was well below his rampaging best.

The Forest defence he had marshalled so magnificently for the last few years was ripped to shreds for the third match in succession by a United side clearly not firing on all cylinders. One fierce free-kick apart, there was not of the usual threat going forward from the player known affectionately as Psycho.

The home game against Liverpool was one of the first big tests of United's championship credentials. Ian Rush's strike just before half-time looked to have buried them again, but the key substitution of Blackmore for Kanchelskis helped United earn a last gasp point.

The emergence of Paul Ince as a
player of true international
class was undoubtedly a factor
in United's success. It was not
just his combative midfield
strength which singled him out.
Superb strikes against QPR and
Crystal Palace away were
crucial goals at vital stages of
the game.

Ooh-ah-Cantona…The transfer was as easy as buying a bar of chocolate, and what a transfer! Within weeks Cantona had established himself as the final piece of Alex Ferguson's jigsaw.

In a season of high drama, Steve Bruce's winner against Sheffield Wednesday deep into injury time was perhaps the most dramatic turning point.

After a Giggs goal of breathtaking quality against Tottenham, George Best, watching from the stands was able to joke, "Maybe they'll soon be talking about me as the second Ryan Giggs." Comparisons were inevitable.

For a manager at Old Trafford, Sir Matt is never far away. Manager of the month awards were two-a-penny for Ferguson. It was the championship that shareholders and supporters demanded.

Cantona's arrival seemed to act as a spur to Mark Hughes. This goal against Norwich was his third winning goal in consecutive games.

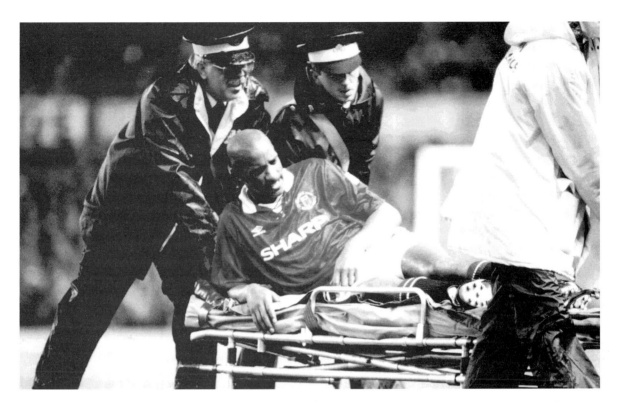

HEARTBREAK: ... Dion Dublin carried off with a broken leg in only his sixth game for United.

Southampton and Nottingham Forest with any real conviction.

Dublin had done little in his front-line liaison with Hughes, and substitute Andrei Kanchelskis' arrival after the break – with Brian McClair switching back into the middle – made little difference.

Peter Schmeichel had already been called into emergency action after 20 minutes when Palace striker Chris Armstrong powered in a close range header that stung the Danish goalkeeper's fingers. And when Schmeichel, under pressure from Mark Bright, lost his grip on a Geoff Thomas header, United Skipper Steve Bruce was there to hack the ball clear from under the bar.

But with the 29,736 crowd melting away towards the exits Hughes delivered the blow that hoisted United into the Premier League's leading pack. The goal owed much to the astute McClair, who turned brilliantly before squaring the ball for Hughes to drill into the Palace net from five yards.

Ferguson said: "I don't think we deserved to win the match but we did deserve something for the way we persevered. We found it very difficult against Palace. They set up a system with five players at the back which was very difficult to break down. But because our defending has improved it gave us a chance of winning it in the last few minutes. This victory gives us a platform from which to launch ourselves."

League Table After Match

	P	W	D	L	F	A	Pts
Norwich	6	4	1	1	13	9	13
Coventry	6	4	0	2	8	6	12
Blackburn	5	3	2	0	7	3	11
QPR	6	3	2	1	8	5	11
Arsenal	6	3	1	2	8	6	10
MAN UTD	6	3	1	2	6	6	10
Everton	5	2	3	0	6	2	9
Leeds	6	2	3	1	13	10	9
Chelsea	6	2	3	1	9	7	9
Ipswich	6	1	5	0	8	7	8
Man City	6	2	2	2	8	8	8
Middlesbrough	5	2	1	2	10	7	7
Oldham	6	1	4	1	12	12	7
Sheff Wed	6	1	3	2	9	9	6
Aston Villa	6	1	3	2	6	7	6
Liverpool	6	1	3	2	7	9	6
Southampton	6	1	3	2	5	7	6
Tottenham	6	1	3	2	5	10	6
C. Palace	6	0	4	2	8	10	4
Sheff Utd	6	1	1	4	7	12	4
Nottm Forest	5	1	0	4	5	12	3
Wimbledon	6	0	2	4	4	8	

September 6

MANCHESTER UNITED 2
LEEDS UNITED 0

(Half-time score: 2-0)

United: Schmeichel, Blackmore, Irwin, Bruce, Ferguson, Pallister, Kanchelskis, Ince, McClair, Hughes, Giggs. Subs: Martin, Walsh, Wallace
Scorers: Kanchelskis 29, Bruce 45
Leeds: Lukic, Fairclough, Newsome (Hodge 67), Whyte, Dorigo, Batty, McAllister, Speed, Rod Wallace (Strachan 15), Chapman, Cantona. Sub: Day
Booked: Fairclough, Newsome
Referee: P Don (Hanworth Park)
Attendance: 31,296
Weather: Breezy

The sweet smell of revenge hung heavily over Old Trafford long after the referee's whistle confirmed Alex Ferguson's first League win against the old enemy. It had taken five months to remove the rancid taste of failure Leeds left in Ferguson's mouth when they snatched away the championship he had coveted all season.

The United boss had heard the story of how Leeds manager Howard Wilkinson dined comfortably at home on roast beef and red wine while Ferguson's side crashed fatally at Liverpool with a week of the programme left. Ferguson needed retribution, especially after dominating the three-game League and Cup series between the two heavyweights at Elland Road the previous mid-winter.

It arrived in the grand manner in a 90-minute live TV exposition that viewers would recognise as Made in Manchester. First-half goals from Andrei Kanchelskis and Steve Bruce sealed Ferguson's first League victory over Leeds in five collisions but there were more, much more, for the Red Hordes to relish.

Mark Hughes could have doubled his season's tally of three goals in a 12-minute second-half spell when everything he touched looked goal-dusted. Paul Ince took the sting from the side which once boasted the best midfield in the Premier League, belying the fact that he was one of three red-shirted players wheezing around with a virus. Ferguson revealed later that Ince, Gary Pallister and Brian McClair were all suffering from the bug sweeping Old Trafford.

The after-match debate between United and England over Ince's availability for the forthcoming midweek international match in Spain was almost as fiercely contested as the conflict on the pitch. The FA assured United that Ince would play in Santander – and if England were looking for the new Bryan Robson then, on this performance, manager Graham Taylor might just have found him.

What had been billed as an intriguing tactical confrontation between Ferguson and Wilkinson turned into a free-wheel by the Manchester club to their fourth successive Premier League victory. At the end the public address system boomed out the Monty Python song United fans adopted as their anthem the night their team beat Barcelona to win the European Cup-winners' Cup in Rotterdam in 1991. "Always look on the bright side of life" they chorused.

Looking on the bright side must have been difficult for Howard Wilkinson. He had switched Chris Fairclough to right-back, with John Newsome in the middle, in an effort to block Ryan Giggs' corridor along the left flank. But Ferguson had already rumbled that ploy and countered it by moving Giggs over to the right and giving Kanchelskis the chance to use his pace against Fairclough.

The manoeuvre worked perfectly after 29 minutes as Denis Irwin fed Giggs. He flung a superb left-footed ball across the penalty area where Kanchelskis came roaring in at the far post to score with a rare header past Leeds goalkeeper John Lukic. By then Gordon Strachan was on for Rod Wallace, whose hamstring injury was expected to keep him out of the Leeds line-up for three weeks.

But apart from one Strachan effort that Peter Schmeichel stopped with his foot, the little guy who used to wow Old Trafford could not make much of a dent. Instead, United captain Bruce dug Leeds into a deeper hole on the stroke of half-time, burying his chance as Irwin's cross slid off Lukic's fist.

Leeds had certainly made a more emphatic start than United and Eric Cantona – then still an Elland Road favourite – did well with one over-the-shoulder effort which flew straight at Schmeichel. But the Yorkshire side could not disturb Ince's combative control in midfield where he was supported valiantly by Darren Ferguson. At 20, the boss's son was doing very nicely, thankyou, and played a full part in United's win.

But the last 25 minutes belonged to Hughes. The Welshman, initially threatened by the arrival of big Dion Dublin, was once more the focal point. He unleashed one shot which crashed against an upright, spread Lukic with another and then saw the big Leeds goalkeeper thwart him again with an outstretched foot.

League Table After Match

	P	W	D	L	F	A	Pts
Norwich	7	5	1	1	14	9	16
Coventry	7	5	0	2	9	6	15
Blackburn	6	4	2	0	11	4	14
MAN UTD	7	4	1	2	8	6	13
QPR	7	3	3	1	8	5	12
Man City	7	3	2	2	11	8	11
Middlesbrough	6	3	1	2	12	7	10
Arsenal	7	3	1	3	10	9	10
Everton	6	2	3	1	7	4	9
Aston Villa	7	2	3	2	9	7	9
Leeds	7	2	3	2	13	12	9
Chelsea	7	2	3	2	10	9	9
Ipswich	7	1	6	0	8	7	9
Liverpool	7	2	3	2	9	10	9
Tottenham	7	2	3	2	7	11	9
Oldham	7	1	4	2	12	13	7
Sheff Wed.	7	1	3	3	9	12	6
Southampton	7	1	3	3	5	8	6
Wimbledon	7	1	2	4	7	10	5
C. Palace	7	0	4	3	8	13	4
Sheff Utd	7	1	1	5	7	14	4
Nottm Forest	6	1	0	5	6	16	3

September 12

EVERTON 0

MANCHESTER UNITED 2

(Half-time score: 2-0)

Everton: Southall, Harper, Watson, Ablett, Hinchcliffe, Warzycha, Horne, Ebbrell (Beagrie 70), Ward, Johnston, Beardsley. Subs: Jackson, Kearton
United: Schmeichel, Irwin, Blackmore, Bruce, Ferguson, Pallister, Kanchelskis, Ince, McClair, Hughes, Giggs. Subs: Martin, Walsh, Wallace
Scorers: McClair 29, Bruce 76 (pen)
Referee: M Peck (Kendall)
Attendance: 30,002
Weather: Overcast

Everton manager Howard Kendall was stunned by the transformation in United in just three-and-half weeks. Kendall had seen the worst and the best of United in a very short space of time. Everton cruised to a 3-0 victory at Old Trafford on August 19 but after rampant United surged into third place in the Premier League with this Goodison victory he admitted: "On that performance United are the best team we have played so far.

"They were solid at the back, quick on the break and skilful in midfield. We were beaten by a better side but, having said that, so many of my players didn't do themselves justice. Their performances fell below the standard required to beat a top side – and United are a top side. We have to be concerned that we have scored only three goals in our last five games."

United's fifth straight League win – courtesy of a Steve Bruce penalty and Brian McClair's first goal of the season – without conceding a goal was their meanest run in top flight football. That run had sent them roaring up the table from the rock bottom situation they found themselves in after that defeat by Everton.

Bruce, United's influential skipper, forged a formidable defensive barrier alongside Gary Pallister and later revealed how Everton had sown the seeds of their own destruction. He said: "We lost our first two games and in the defeat by Everton we made stupid mistakes. When you lose heavily like that you just have to put things right and that is how it's proved. We went back to working hard and concentrating on the basics.

"Now we're looking like a team again. The whole side can take credit for the way we're defending and we all know what a good goalkeeper we have in Peter Schmeichel. If we don't stop them he's there and doing the job well. It's always pleasing not to concede goals and if we keep it tight at the back we've got a chance of winning the League."

With players like Danny Wallace, Neil Webb and Lee Martin not even in their starting line-up United were beginning to look a formidable force once more. Bruce added: "When you look at the people who aren't playing in the team you realise the depth of quality we have."

Peter Beardsley, so often Everton's inspiration, blamed himself for spurning an early second-half chance after Schmeichel had saved his initial shot. His miss, and another by Mo Johnston, ensured a new entry in the Old Trafford record books. The only other time United had won five successive League matches without conceding a goal was pre-war in the Second Division.

League Table After Match

	P	W	D	L	F	A	Pts
Norwich	8	6	1	1	17	11	19
Blackburn	7	5	2	0	12	4	17
MAN UTD	8	5	1	2	10	6	16
QPR	8	4	3	1	10	6	15
Coventry	7	5	0	2	9	6	15
Middlesbrough	7	4	1	2	13	7	13
Ipswich	8	2	6	0	10	8	12
Man City	8	3	2	3	11	9	11
Arsenal	8	3	1	4	10	10	10
Aston Villa	7	2	3	2	9	7	9
Leeds	7	2	3	2	13	12	9
Everton	7	2	3	2	7	6	9
Chelsea	8	2	3	3	12	12	9
Sheff Wed.	8	2	3	3	11	13	9
Liverpool	8	2	3	3	9	11	9
Tottenham	7	2	3	2	7	11	9
Oldham	8	1	5	2	14	15	8
Sheff Utd	8	2	1	5	8	14	7
Southampton	8	1	3	4	6	10	6
Wimbledon	8	1	2	5	8	12	5
C. Palace	8	0	5	3	10	15	5
Nottm Forest	7	1	0	6	7	18	3

September 19

TOTTENHAM 1

MANCHESTER UNITED 1

(Half-time score: 0-1)

Spurs: Walker, Austin (Tuttle 45), Cundy, Ruddock, Van den Hauwe, Turner, Gray (Hendry 62), Sedgeley, Allen, Durie, Sheringham. Sub: Thorsvedt
Scorer: Durie 52
Booked: Durie
United: Schmeichel, Irwin, Blackmore, Bruce, Ferguson, Pallister, Kanchelskis (Wallace 74), Ince, McClair, Hughes, Giggs. Subs: Martin, Walsh
Scorer: Giggs 45
Booked: Bruce
Referee: R Groves (Weston-Super-Mare)
Attendance: 33,296
Weather: Calm

Just when they needed it most United turned in the kind of performance which left no question as to their pedigree. Three days earlier United were held to a goalless draw at Old Trafford by the £4-a-week players of Torpedo Moscow in the UEFA Cup first round, first leg.

Critics were quick to resurrect doubts about their quality but Alex Ferguson's usual line-up had been shot full of holes. Injuries and UEFA restrictions meant that 11 possible first-team players were unavailable. But at White Hart Lane the real United came out to play.

Only Tottenham's hard work and determination – and an equaliser from Gordon Durie – prevented United from chalking up six Premier League victories on the trot. Fergie looked a contented man once again although his defence had their moments of anxiety in the face of Spurs' spirited challenge.

Paul Ince was clearly maturing into a reliable all-purpose midfielder soon to stake a claim to a regular England place. And then there was Ryan Giggs. He produced the sort of display that gave everyone but dyed-in-the-wool Spurs fans a thrill in the knowledge that they had witnessed an emerging talent of staggering proportions.

Even George Best saw a reflection of his own glory days in the way Giggs, still only 18, stole the ball, pushed it between a defender's legs, dragged it clear of the goalkeeper and then threaded his shot into the net from a difficult angle.

Spurs coach Doug Livermore was just the latest in a growing line of football opponents unable to hide his admiration. "Giggs has tremendous quality," enthused Livermore. "A great left foot, pace, crossing ability and finishing. But he also has another dimension – he's good when he hadn't got the ball. I worked with Ian Rush at Chester and at international level. Giggs reminds me of him in that he won't let people settle.

"He pinched a ball today that a lot of players would have given up. He puts defenders under pressure expecting them to make mistakes. It's a terrific asset."

But manager Ferguson was still determined not to let Giggs' burgeoning status as United's star attraction go to his head, refusing to remove the "handle with care" sticker. "He's had a really good start, although there were problems against Crystal Palace, who really man-marked him," said Fergie. "But that is part of his learning process. He didn't play against Moscow so we could do some coaching on him and I think he benefited from it.

"The problem is that you are playing him all the time when, at 18, you should be training and coaching him. Because of the number of games you don't often get the chance but we'll find the moments and rest him. Just now he's still fresh and fit. Ryan is getting stronger but physique is not a problem because he has such good balance. In the winter, when the grounds are heavy, is when we'll rest him."

Ferguson then paid tribute to Spurs, who looked to have recovered impressively after a 5-0 defeat by Leeds earlier in the season. Ferguson said: "They have lost Paul Gascoigne, Gary Lineker and Paul Stewart. It has meant big chances for them, and they have had to start building again.

"They earned this draw out of honesty and hard work … and they are not bad qualities when you are trying to get yourself back among the elite. On what I've seen here no-one is going to come to White Hart Lane and find it easy."

Above: BLOOD BROTHER … Giggs sheds a drop in the cause.

Left: McClair shoots through the massesd Spurs defence.

League Table After Match

	P	W	D	L	F	A	Pts
Norwich	9	7	1	1	18	11	22
Blackburn	9	5	3	1	15	8	18
Coventry	8	6	0	2	10	6	18
MAN UTD	9	5	2	2	11	7	17
QPR	9	4	4	1	13	9	15
Middlesbrough	8	4	2	2	16	10	14
Aston Villa	9	3	4	2	14	10	13
Ipswich	9	2	6	1	12	12	12
Everton	9	3	3	3	10	10	12
Man City	8	3	2	3	11	9	11
Oldham	9	2	5	2	18	17	11
Leeds	9	2	5	2	15	14	11
Arsenal	9	3	2	4	11	11	11
Tottenham	9	2	4	3	8	13	10
Chelsea	8	2	3	3	12	12	9
Sheff Wed.	9	2	3	4	11	14	9
Liverpool	9	2	3	4	11	15	9
C. Palace	9	1	5	3	12	15	8
Sheff Utd	9	2	2	5	9	15	8
Southampton	9	1	4	4	7	11	7
Wimbledon	9	1	3	5	9	13	6
Nottm Forest	7	1	0	6	7	18	3

September 26

MANCHESTER UNITED 0

QUEEN'S PARK RANGERS 0

(Half-time score: 0-0)

United: Schmeichel, Irwin, Blackmore, Bruce, Ferguson, Pallister, Kanchelskis (Wallace 77), Ince, McClair, Hughes, Giggs. Subs: Martin, Walsh
Booked: Ince
QPR: Stejskal, Bardsley, Peacock, Maddix, Brevett, Impey, Wilkins, Holloway, Sinton, Ferdinand (Barker 53), Penrice. Subs: Channing, Roberts
Referee: D Allison (Lancaster)
Attendance: 33,287
Weather: Warm

Goals started to dry up as United battled through three tough matches in the space of a week. Danny Wallace, United's former England winger, stepped briefly from the shadows of the Central League team to score a brilliant goal at the Goldstone Ground to give United a 1-1 draw with Brighton in the Coca-Cola Cup second round, first leg.

But a week later United's European hopes were shattered in Russia. Mark Hughes was sent off two minutes from the end of normal time for his second booking and although 10-man United stood firm in extra-time they went out on penalties – Brian McClair, Gary Pallister and Steve Bruce all missing from the spot.

The Premier League clash with Queens Park Rangers, sandwiched in between, was almost as disappointing. Despite controlling so much of the match United lacked the guile and the cutting edge to turn territorial advantage into goals. It was the same old problem. After failing to buy Alan Shearer from Southampton and then losing Dion Dublin so tragically, United's attack was not so much a rapier as a blunt instrument.

Alex Ferguson was clearly disappointed that his side had failed to avenge the 4-1 thrashing United suffered at the hands of QPR on the first day of 1992. "Rangers came for a point and it was up to us to break them down," he admitted. "We didn't sustain the pressure. If we'd have got one goal it would have opened the door."

Even without defensive leader Alan McDonald, Rangers had enough organisation and shape to repel United raids that lost their sting on the 18-yard line. In fact, only a brilliant second-half save by goalkeeper Peter Schmeichel prevented Rangers from taking all three points. Andrew Impey teed up Gary Penrice but Schmeichel managed to turn his ferocious drive over the bar.

United's best chance fell to Hughes, who exchanged a first-half one-two with Brian McClair but saw Jan Stejskal get down well to save. Hughes had a chance to make amends after Paul Ince's shot was blocked but once again Stejskal saved well.

United had begun brightly and Ryan Giggs caused several moments of near-panic before Rangers' defence settled down and took control. And when McClair released Andrei Kanchelskis on the

*WING WONDER ...
Kanchelskis sets up
another attack.*

right, the Ukrainian skipped over Darren Peacock's lunging tackle only to direct his cross too close to the goalkeeper. After the break Schmeichel's accurate thrown clearance found McClair who again released Kanchelskis on the right. He cut in smartly and seemed to have done everything right but his shot skidded across the face of the goal to safety.

October 3

The bookies were convinced, opponents Boro were impressed and United's players maintained a rigid self-belief.

But the bottom line in football is goals and while United weren't exactly in debit during a dogged autumn, the scoring balance sheet did not make good reading either.

The men from Manchester rounded off a rotten week and began a rotten month with this draw at Ayresome Park that seemed typical United: pressure, panache, thrills, spills … and just one goal – and that a penalty.

United produced some moments of superb quality and there were times when Ryan Giggs looked unplayable. On occasion, it looked as though United couldn't have failed to win the match if they had tried.

Twice United front-runners – Mark Hughes and then Giggs – managed to round Middlesbrough keeper Ian Ironside and couldn't finish.

Still, United were sitting pretty after Steve Bruce – who had failed from the spot during the shoot-out in Moscow in the Cup Winners' Cup earlier in the week – rediscovered his sure penalty touch.

But Bernie Slaven capped a stirring Boro second-half revival to show just what proven goalscorers are all about. Mike Phelan, caught out in the wet, allowed Chris Morris' free kick to skid through his legs and Irish international Slaven pounced, slotting home past Peter Schmeichel.

The result did not disturb the bookies too much and, while hedging their bets with proven stayers Arsenal, believed United at 3-1 were still the best tip for the title.

And Slaven was suitably impressed by the quality of their claims, saying: "I would say Aston Villa are the best side we have come up against so far, but United aren't far behind.

"They are certainly as good as last year, they'll compete well for the title, a great side on the break. One minute you are attacking, then you look up and they're gone."

Boro boss Lennie Lawrence also admitted: "They cut us to pieces." And even though Hughes missed two easy chances, Bruce maintained the players' united front when he said: "We aren't going to get paranoid. We're going to get on with it.

"Maybe one day soon we are going to go out and hit somebody with six or seven, but at the moment it's just not happening for us.

"We are playing well, creating chances, but just not sticking them away. If the luck is against you, there's not much you can do. I think we showed again what a good side we are and I think pretty soon we are going to give someone a real hiding."

For Hughes – sent off in the Euro defeat in Moscow and taken off here to give Bryan Robson a 20-minute run-out – that day could not come soon enough. Added Bruce: "Knowing Sparky, he will bounce back next week and maybe get us three."

Bryan Robson outpaces the Middlesbrough defence.

League Table After Match

	P	W	D	L	F	A	Pts
Blackburn	11	7	3	1	24	9	24
Norwich	11	7	2	2	20	19	23
Coventry	11	6	3	2	14	10	21
QPR	11	5	5	1	17	10	20
Aston Villa	11	5	4	2	20	14	19
MAN UTD	11	5	4	1	12	8	19
Arsenal	11	5	2	4	14	12	17
Ipswich	11	3	7	1	16	14	16
Middlesbrough	10	4	3	3	19	14	15
Leeds	11	3	5	3	19	18	14
Chelsea	11	3	4	4	14	14	13
Man City	11	3	3	5	13	13	12
Sheff Wed	11	3	3	5	13	15	12
Everton	10	3	3	4	10	12	12
Liverpool	11	3	3	5	14	18	12
Sheff Utd	11	3	3	5	11	15	12
Oldham	10	2	5	3	18	19	11
Southampton	11	2	4	5	9	14	10
Tottenham	11	2	4	5	9	19	10
C. Palace	11	1	6	4	15	19	9
Wimbledon	11	2	3	6	14	18	9
Nottm Forest	10	1	3	6	10	21	6

October 18

MANCHESTER UNITED 1

LIVERPOOL 2

(Half-time score: 2-2)

United: Schmeichel, Parker, Irwin, Bruce, Ferguson, Pallister, Kanchelskis (Blackmore 66), Ince, McClair, Hughes, Giggs. Subs: Phelan
Scorer: Hughes 78, 90
Liverpool: Grobbelaar, Marsh, Piechnik, Nicol, Burrows, Hutchison, Molby (Tanner 82), Redknapp (Thomas 72), McManaman, Rush, Rosenthal. Sub: James
Scorers: Hutchison 23, Rush 44
Booked: Rush
Referee: K Hackett (Sheffield)
Attendance: 33,243
Weather: Cool

There were just seconds left and many in the 33,243 crowd had decided that was it.

Defeat loomed, the spectre of yet more false hopes dashed hung round Old Trafford – and all to United's deadliest rivals from the other end of the East Lancs Road.

It just had to be Liverpool, didn't it, you could hear the fans say as they began to trudge away to their cars and buses. Liverpool, the club who had won titles seemingly at will while United endured seasons of failure. Liverpool, who always seemed to have what it takes to claim the big prize. Liverpool, who had Ian Rush and who had tormented United once again.

And despite Mark Hughes at last finding his touch in front of goal ten minutes earlier, it seemed to be small consolation following Liverpool's second goal from his fellow Welsh international, Rush. The 287th strike of Rush's career made him Liverpool's record goalscorer, overhauling Roger Hunt's tally of 23 years ago.

Until the last quarter United were second best to a Liverpool side guided by youngsters Jamie Redknapp and Don Hutchison.

Israeli international Ronny Rosenthal had caused United no end of problems before Graeme Souness's side got the break their football deserved after 23 minutes.

Don Hutchison's 25-yard shot looked harmless, but it spun off Steve Bruce and deflected into the net past Peter Schmeichel. And when Rosenthal laid on the second for Rush to score his record-making goal on half-time, his first in a League game at Old Trafford, the game looked lost for United.

United manager's son Darren Ferguson had wasted two early chances and Ryan Giggs put the frighteners on Liverpool three minutes into the second half from Ferguson's through ball. But again the excellent Bruce Grobbelaar was one move ahead to give him no angle and make the save.

Then in the 78th minute Clayton Blackmore, a substitute for Kanchelskis, lifted the ball towards Hughes. The Welshman's spectacular volley from outside the area left Grobbelaar standing.

But as the final seconds ticked away, fans turned on their heels

sensing a dramatic climax. Young Giggs – another Welshman –
again broke down the left and whipped in a cross.

And as those fans stood transfixed, unmoving, scarcely
breathing, Hughes, striking like a cobra, launched himself at the
ball, met it sweetly and struck right at the heart of Liverpool's goal.
There was an almost imperceptible millisecond of hesitation born of
disbelief and then the ground erupted. Grown men flung their arms
to the skies and Hughes was buried under the weight of his team-
mates' relief.

WHAT A DIVE …
Mark Hughes scores the
winner against Liverpool.

How sweet to deny Liverpool. How ironic that the one team who
had made a speciality of saving or winning games at the death,
should themselves be subject to one final coup de grâce.

It was a theme United were to return to throughout the season.
And against Liverpool, it was perhaps the first time United's players
had displayed a championship-winning will to win that was forged
in the furnace of failure the season before.

Hughes said of Rush later: "Ian's scoring record is its own tribute
to his quality. For the past decade he has been the best in the
country. People say I don't score enough and I accept that criticism
to some extent. But the role I play doesn't help. Maybe I need to get
into the box a bit more."

The two goals capped the end of a turbulent time for Hughes –
sent off in Moscow, substituted against Middlesbrough and then a
World Cup winner for Wales in Cyprus a few days before this match.

Rival boss Graeme Souness acknowledged United's fightback but wasn't happy, saying: "In the end our inexperience cost us two extra points. We played well and our youngsters were disappointed. I thought Bruce Grobbelaar came a bit too far for the first Hughes goal and that started their comeback. Bruce found himself in no man's land."

Rush said after: "I'm proud and privileged to have beaten the record of such a great Liverpool player as Roger Hunt. He was my father's hero. My dad used to call him Sir Roger. But while it's nice to have the record, I would rather the side had achieved the win we deserved."

Alex Ferguson was not going to go that far in praising Liverpool, but he did admit: "They were first to the ball and deserved their 2-0 half-time lead. I felt for much of the game we were sluggish after having so many players away for midweek internationals.

"We need a goal to inspire us and we looked like the real United in the last 15 minutes."

And perhaps, he might have added, the real United play to the finish these days.

League Table After Match

	P	W	D	L	F	A	Pts
Norwich	12	8	2	2	22	20	26
Blackburn	11	7	3	1	24	9	24
Coventry	12	6	4	2	15	11	22
QPR	12	5	5	2	18	12	20
MAN UTD	12	5	5	2	14	10	20
Arsenal	12	6	2	4	15	12	20
Aston Villa	11	5	4	2	20	14	19
Leeds	12	4	5	3	22	19	17
Middlesbrough	11	4	4	3	21	16	16
Ipswich	12	3	7	2	17	16	16
Chelsea	12	4	4	4	16	15	16
Sheff Wed.	12	4	3	5	15	16	15
Oldham	12	3	5	4	20	21	14
Man City	12	3	4	5	13	13	13
Everton	12	3	4	5	11	14	13
Liverpool	12	3	4	5	16	20	13
Sheff Utd	12	3	3	6	12	18	12
Southampton	12	2	5	5	11	16	11
Tottenham	12	2	5	5	11	21	11
Wimbledon	12	2	4	6	16	20	10
C. Palace	12	1	7	4	15	19	10
Nottm Forest	11	1	3	7	10	22	6

October 24

Wherever Manchester United go and whatever they do, it seems they are always pursued by some ghost or other.

This season of triumph ultimately buried so many ghosts for the men from Old Trafford, but on October 24 1992 the haunted look on the face of the famous old club was creased by a few more lines.

First, since the draw with Liverpool the previous Sunday, Alex Ferguson had had to deal with the fall-out from the wrangle over Neil Webb. Bought from Nottingham Forest for £1.5 million in the early optimistic days of Ferguson's reign and trumpeted as the man who, alongside Bryan Robson, would form a dream midfield ticket for England and United, Webb became Fergie's problem child.

An Achilles injury saw Webb lose his England place and despite a noble fightback to full health, he never fulfilled the promise that Ferguson had hoped he would in Manchester.

The two men fell out and, less than two weeks before this match, Webb's journalist wife Shelley underlined on TV the rift between manager and star by publicly criticising Ferguson for his comments about players in his new book.

And the end for Webb was signalled when it was revealed he had been fined a week's wages – around £3000 – by United for a drink episode. Despite mediation from players' union chief Gordon Taylor, it became obvious that a split was unavoidable and a move back to Forest inevitable.

Webb had the substantial sum docked from his pay packet because of an incident on the night of United's Sky TV game at Southampton on August 24. Ferguson was reported to be annoyed with Webb on arrival at the team hotel and sent him home the next morning. He was fined two weeks' wages, but had the fine halved on appeal.

Ferguson said: "I will not talk about an internal disciplinary matter concerning one of my players beyond saying we wouldn't be fining a player two weeks' wages for a minor incident."

It seemed just another torment Fergie could do without as he attempted to keep United on an even course during a stormy autumn.

And the last thing he could have wanted was a trip to the nouveaux riches of Blackburn. Rovers had spent, spent, spent in an

BLCKBURN 0
_____

MANCHESTER UNITED 0
(Half-time score: 0-0)

Blackburn: Mimms, May, Moran, Hendry, Wright, Ripley (Wegere 80), Cowans, Sherwood, Wilcox, Newell, Shearer. Subs: Marker, Collier
Booked: Sherwood
United: Schmeichel, Parker, Irwin, Bruce, Ferguson (Kanchelskis 75), Pallister, Blackmore, Ince, McClair, Hughes, Giggs. Subs: Walsh, Webb
Booked: Bruce, Blackmore
Referee: M Reed (Birmingham)
Attendance: 20,305
Weather: Warm

effort to sit at the same table as aristocrats such as Manchester United.

And worse, backed by the steel fortune of magnate Jack Walker and the 24-carat management of Kenny Dalglish, Rovers had flaunted their new found wealth and status by snatching England's hottest striking prospect Alan Shearer from under the considerable charms of their big city, big time neighbours.

And how it must have showed that October day at Ewood Park. For United, it must have been like being invited round to the new residents on Mahogany Row and told: "Let me show you our new Ferrari. There's only one of its kind in the country. Only three million quid or so. Isn't it right you wanted to buy it …?"

And how it must have gnawed at United fans as they saw game after game in those early season days, saw United fail to score and then read the next day: "If only United could have persuaded Shearer to go to Old Trafford.". And that statement was usually followed by the whisper: "Yes, but they wouldn't pay the money …"

Manchester United? Not enough money? Surely not. But, as Shearer was piling in the goals last autumn, Ferguson would have had to have the good grace of a saint, never mind an ex-Saint like Shearer, not to have privately fretted that he could not capture the signature of the former Southampton star.

And here Shearer was. Another ghost to haunt a club beset by ghosts. The United fans, naturally, tormented the England star throughout a goalless afternoon while Steve Bruce and Gary Pallister concentrated on subduing him.

MY BALL …
Gary Pallister and
Alan Shearer in a tussle.

But Dalglish maintained: "Shearer was goaded about money, but even if everything had been equal in the bids he would still have come here. Alan did not come here for the money nor did anyone else. If that was the sole object of coming to Blackburn Rovers he would not have been asked."

Money may or may not have come into the equation when Dalglish was persuaded off the golf course but he had performed a miracle at Rovers. Alan Hansen suggested on television that if United had persuaded Shearer to go to Old Trafford we would have been discussing even then who would be coming second in the Premier League.

And Ferguson, straight, old-fashioned, did say: "We are not searching for form but someone to put the ball in the onion bag. We don't worry so much about who is going to score against us as who is going to score for us."

But then there was another ghost of Old Trafford past haunting Fergie at Ewood. United were prevented from scoring largely because of one Kevin Moran. Moran, 36 then, a dogged Dubliner who had earned all his battle colours for United, even earning the notoriety of being sent off at Wembley in their cause . . . and released by Ferguson.

The Republic of Ireland international did not have too much to say of Fergie, but this season he has certainly made a point to those who thought him finished as a big league central defender. About Dalglish, he said: "He has that air of authority about him. He doesn't rant and rave. He encourages you to play football and be positive. He commands respect for what he achieved as a player and a manager before he came here."

Yes, it was an afternoon when United were reminded too often about too many things they would maybe rather have forgotten.

At least Shearer had the grace not to score. But you could not ignore him, especially when he earned a blast from United goal-keeper Peter Schmeichel for a penalty box challenge.

And you could not ignore Rovers.

They went top of the league that day.

League Table After Match

	P	W	D	L	F	A	Pts
Blackburn	13	7	5	1	24	9	26
Norwich	12	8	2	2	22	20	26
QPR	13	6	5	2	20	13	23
Arsenal	13	7	2	4	17	12	23
Coventry	13	6	4	3	16	13	22
Aston Villa	13	5	6	2	21	15	21
MAN UTD	13	5	6	2	14	10	21
Chelsea	13	5	4	4	18	16	19
Middlesbrough	13	4	5	4	22	18	17
Leeds	13	4	5	4	23	21	17
Ipswich	13	3	8	2	19	18	17
Man City	13	4	4	5	14	13	16
Sheff Wed.	13	4	4	5	16	17	16
Oldham	13	3	6	4	21	22	15
Liverpool	12	3	4	5	16	20	13
Everton	13	3	4	6	11	16	13
Sheff Utd	13	3	4	6	12	18	13
C. Palace	13	1	8	4	17	21	11
Southampton	13	2	5	6	11	17	11
Tottenham	12	2	5	5	11	21	11
Wimbledon	12	2	4	6	16	20	10
Nottm Forest	13	2	4	7	11	22	10

October 31

MANCHESTER UNITED 1

WIMBLEDON 1

(Half-time score: 0-0)

United: Schmeichel, Parker, Blackmore, Bruce, Ferguson, Pallister, Kanchelskis (Robson 67), Ince, McClair, Hughes, Giggs. Subs: Phelan, Walsh
Booked: Ferguson
Wimbledon: Segers, Barton, McLeary, McAllister, Joseph, Gibson, Jones, Earle, Sanchez, Dobbs (Clarke 82), Holdsworth. Subs: Sullivan, Cotterill
Scorer: Sanchez 79
Booked: Gibson, McAllister, Sanchez
Referee: K Morton (Bury St Edmunds)
Attendance: 32,622
Weather: Sunny

The autumn leaves were falling and so were United's chances of winning anything – like a stone.

And following a disappointing Coca Cola Cup exit to arch-rivals Aston Villa in midweek, defeat to Wimbledon sparked dark mutterings that Alex Ferguson might not see in the New Year as United boss.

The previous season, wise old commentators had seen United's triumph in the Old League Cup, toppling Leeds on the way to a Wembley win over Forest, and success over Leeds again in the FA Cup, as their downfall on the championship campaign trail.

After all, Leeds, without any distractions and, crucially, without any fixture pile-up, had gone on to snatch the title from a fast-fading United.

But if those same experts had seen a glimmer of hope in United's cup defeat to Villa, they would have been choking on their lagers following the plundering of points by those pirates of the Premier League, Wimbledon.

It was the end of a trying month for the Reds. Don't anyone ever invite Alex Ferguson to an Octoberfest.

The Villa reverse was United's first defeat in England since losing to Everton back in August. But the flip side of that run, after crashing to the Dons, was just one victory in the last 11 games.

And trophies do have the habit of being won by sides who score goals. So the most worrying statistic of all that presented itself to Ferguson then was just 16 goals in 19 games. Added to that, against Wimbledon, United did not look like scoring.

At Villa Park, they were beaten by a strike from a proven goal-scorer – Dean Saunders. And while Laurie Sanchez would admit he is not a scoring giant, the Wimbledon mid-fielder has a habit of doing a David act to Goliaths.

It was his goal that brought the downfall of Liverpool in a memorable 1988 FA Cup final, and 11 minutes from time at Old Trafford, he skimmed in Terry Gibson's free kick to seal a deserved Dons victory.

It prompted a rave-up – a ghetto-blaster, naked Vinnie Jones and all – from the Wimbledon players in their dressing room after the match, and it mocked an eerie quiet from United just up the corridor.

Alex Ferguson did not need to be told what it means to a team – especially a bunch of waifs like the Wimbledon team – to win at the Theatre of Dreams, but Dons manager Joe Kinnear thought he'd say so anyway.

"The lads celebrated in the same way when they won at Liverpool. They're a boisterous lot, but still a lovely bunch. They see it as a great achievement coming to the home of one of the big boys and winning."

But once again, the underlying theme for United was goal starvation that was turning into a famine.

It took 76 minutes of this match – it happened to be Paul Ince – to test the athletic Hans Segers. But on this showing you would not have backed anyone on the Old Trafford payroll to hit a barndoor with a howitzer.

Manager Ferguson likened this embarrassment to the Manchurian Candidate syndrome … the insidious drip, drip, drip of a finishing problem that was becoming ingrained on the United psyche.

Mark Hughes' frequent isolation up front seemed to say much about the problem and even without top-scorer John Fashanu, Wimbledon seemed to have more ideas and character than an increasingly neurotic United.

Fergie had turned his worldwide search for a striker to Norway by then and the elegantly named Tore Andre Dahlum was to be given a trial at United.

But for the 32,622 who slunk out of Old Trafford that afternoon, the whole season was starting to turn into something of a trial.

Hughes goes through a mêlée of defenders.

League Table After Match

	P	W	D	L	F	A	Pts
Blackburn	14	7	6	1	24	9	27
Norwich	14	8	3	3	24	25	27
QPR	13	6	5	2	20	13	23
Arsenal	13	7	2	4	17	12	23
Coventry	14	6	5	3	18	15	23
Aston Villa	13	5	6	2	21	15	21
MAN UTD	14	5	6	3	14	11	21
Ipswich	14	4	8	2	20	18	20
Man City	14	5	4	5	17	14	19
Chelsea	14	5	4	5	19	18	19
Middlesbrough	14	4	6	4	23	19	18
Leeds	14	4	6	4	25	23	18
Sheff Wed	14	4	5	5	16	17	17
Liverpool	14	4	4	6	20	23	16
Sheff Utd	14	4	4	6	14	19	16
Oldham	14	3	6	5	21	23	15
Tottenham	14	3	6	5	14	22	15
Wimbledon	14	3	5	6	18	21	14
Southampton	14	3	5	6	12	17	14
Everton	14	3	4	7	12	19	13
C Palace	13	1	8	4	17	21	11
Nottm Forest	14	2	4	8	11	23	10

November 7

ASTON VILLA **1**

MANCHESTER UNITED **0**

(Half-time score: 1-0)

Villa: Spink, Barrett, Small, McGrath, Teale, Staunton, Richardson, Houghton, Parker, Atkinson, Saunders. Subs: Yorke, Bosnich, Regis
Scorer: Atkinson 12
United: Schmeichel, Parker, Blackmore, Bruce, Ferguson (McClair 80), Pallister, Robson, Ince, Sharpe, Hughes, Giggs. Subs: Digby, Kanchelskis
Booked: Robson
Referee: D Elleray (Harrow)
Attendance: 39,063
Weather: Fine

The name Atkinson would probably be a dirty word round Old Trafford now had Aston Villa gone on to deny United the title. At Villa Park on November 7, it took on a double meaning that just wasn't funny.

First it was Dalian Atkinson who expertly scored the winning goal and then went on to explain just why United were not at that stage championship contenders.

Then, of course, it was Ron Atkinson, Big Ron, from his days in Manchester. And here he was, on the sixth anniversary of his leaving United, having produced a side playing with the style he had brought to Old Trafford and a side which even then were looking the best of the bunch to challenge the League's new leaders, Arsenal.

But if Doctor Dalian was dispensing advice this time, then the prescription remained the same as it had been in the weeks previously.

Dalian, took time, following his starring role, to offer the hand of sympathy to co-member Mark Hughes.

Hughes had once again campaigned in not so splendid isolation up front and been given the task of scoring goals for a team in which confidence and aggression were in as short supply as wine at a teetotallers' wedding.

"I feel sorry for Hughes," said Atkinson junior. "He's up there battling away and doing the job I do for Villa, but there's no one around to help.

"He's crying out for support. He needs someone like I've got in Dean Saunders. Until he gets it, Manchester United aren't going to realise their potential and for them that must mean being in the chase for the title.

"Mark Hughes is having it tough, but the fans aren't getting at him because they realise how difficult it is for him. I had a nightmare last season with Villa. Even now, I can get better.

"I'd say I'm operating at 82 per cent efficiencyat the moment. When I can go past players for fun, when I can do it without thinking and look back at them trailing after me, that's when I'll know I'm back to my best."

Villa were exciting and fluent and in Steve Staunton, who was moved up from defence to midfield, had a real star performer as Atkinson set them on their way with his 12th minute strike.

And it might have been more, but for the massive presence of Peter Schmeichel in United's goal. "He's so big, so difficult to get the ball past," said Dalian Atkinson.

UP AND AWAY …
Villa's Dalian Atkinson jumps over Peter Schmeichel as he scores the winner.

And Paul McGrath, a former member of a United team under Ron Atkinson that did its best to uphold the Old Trafford footballing tradition and yet flattered to deceive when it came to winning the League, admitted: "It gets me down a bit when I see United not doing so well because I spent happy years there."

And McGrath, who had had a public feud with United boss Alex Ferguson through the newspapers, added: "They will need a couple of changes and then they will improve. But get back into the League picture? I don't know about that."

This defeat meant United had not won a League game since September 12 (against Everton) and had not scored in four games since Hughes got them out of trouble so memorably against Liverpool. And that stood in stark contrast to Ron Atkinson's Villa, unbeaten in 12 games and playing with all the elan that we had come to know so well of old Bojangles.

Indeed it was a painful contrast that people were making between Ron and his successor at Old Trafford, Alex Ferguson. Fergie had been criticised the previous season for allowing an apparently sullen, worried outlook to permeate through the ranks of his players. You smile, so the theory went, and your players played like they enjoyed it. You scowl and worry and your players fret through a game, hardly daring to make a mistake lest they add to the gloom.

And it was being said that as Villa reflected their laugh-a-day, knockabout, raconteur of a boss, so United – functional, tough to beat, but not the kind of side to take to a party – were an image of their manager. Or so the theory went…

But little did Dalian, Ron or any other Atkinson know at the time, but this match was to mark a watershed for United.

It would be the last time United were to lose in the League for nearly two months. And it would be the last time anyone would suggest that this Manchester United did not play with style.

League Table After Match

	P	W	D	L	F	A	Pts
Arsenal	15	9	2	4	22	13	29
Blackburn	15	7	6	2	24	11	27
Aston Villa	15	7	6	2	24	15	27
Norwich	14	8	3	3	24	25	27
QPR	15	7	5	3	22	15	26
Coventry	15	6	5	4	18	18	23
Man City	15	6	4	5	21	14	22
Chelsea	15	6	4	5	22	19	22
Ipswich	15	4	9	2	20	18	21
MAN UTD	15	5	6	4	14	12	21
Liverpool	15	5	4	6	24	24	19
Middlesbrough	15	4	6	5	24	23	18
Leeds	15	4	6	5	25	27	18
Tottenham	15	4	6	5	16	22	18
Sheff Wed	14	4	5	5	16	17	17
Sheff Utd	14	4	4	6	14	19	16
Everton	15	4	4	7	13	19	16
Oldham	14	3	6	5	21	23	15
Southampton	15	3	6	6	12	17	15
Wimbledon	15	3	5	7	18	23	14
C. Palace	15	1	8	6	19	26	11
Nottm Forest	15	2	4	9	11	24	10

NO WAY THROUGH … Dean Saunders loses out to Darren Ferguson and Paul Ince.

November 21

"It was a good day for us," enthused United boss Alex Ferguson. He could say that again.

Not only would this victory mark the beginning of a serious assault on the summit of the Premier League, it signalled the end of a few troubled days for the manager.

Fergie, searching for the firepower to spark that assault, had turned once again to Sheffield Wednesday's £4 million-rated England man David Hirst. News of his bid for the coltish striker found no favour with Sheffield Wednesday manager Trevor Francis.

Hirst stayed – through choice, and through Francis's threat to quit if his star man was sold. Fergie had to keep his own counsel for fear of fuelling an already public row.

But even the good intent behind the move wasn't enough to placate United's shareholders who, 24 hours before this match, had given the Old Trafford board and by implication the management, a stormy time at their annual meeting.

What was the point, they argued, of Manchester United Plc showing a healthy profit, if Manchester United FC continued to suffer a playing loss?

Forget the Footsie; what about the Football?

So it was indeed a good afternoon to calm those protests, if not silence them completely.

Given a benevolent Oldham defence, United recorded their first win in the League for two months and, just as significantly after a barren run in front of goal, scored three times in a competitive match for the first time since the season began.

United demolished Oldham within half an hour with Brian McClair and Mark Hughes – showing understanding and urgency together – swinging the big iron ball up front.

Bryan Robson and Paul Ince dominated midfield while Lee Sharpe and Ryan Giggs provided pace, skill and width to which Oldham could find no answer.

Nine days earlier, United had hinted on a freezing night in Manchester that they were ready to come in from the cold. Playing Danish aces Brondby in a friendly, United had popped in three goals then too, with Scotsman McClair, having earlier been axed by

MANCHESTER UNITED 3

OLDHAM 0

(Half-time score: 3-0)

United: Schmeichel, Parker, Irwin (Phelan 77), Bruce, Sharpe, Pallister, Robson, Ince (Butt 65), McClair, Hughes, Giggs.
Sub: Digby
Scorers: McClair 10, 28, Hughes 11
Oldham: Hallworth, Halle, Redmond, Jobson, Pointon, Milligan, Henry, McDonald, Adams, Marshall, Sharpe (Olney 62). Subs: Bernard, Gerrard
Booked: Adams, Jobson
Referee: A Gunn (South Chailey)
Attendance: 33,497
Weather: Wet

HOT SHOT … Brian McClair cracks home the first goal against Oldham.

club and country, returning to the scoring form that put him top of the Old Trafford goal charts when he arrived from Celtic in June 1987 for £850,000.

So it was fitting that against Oldham it was McClair who knocked in United's first goal after ten minutes from Giggs' cross before Hughes drove a shot through the goalkeeper's legs from Ince's pass 60 seconds later.

McClair scored his second after 28 minutes from Steve Bruce's backheel, before United took their foot off the accelerator.

But on the road to the championship, it was a good day indeed and a great way to start a trip to glory.

League Table After Match

	P	W	D	L	F	A	Pts
Norwich	16	10	3	3	29	28	33
Arsenal	16	9	2	5	22	16	29
Aston Villa	16	7	7	2	24	15	28
Blackburn	15	7	6	2	24	11	27
QPR	15	7	5	3	22	15	26
Man City	16	7	4	5	24	16	25
Chelsea	16	7	4	5	23	19	25
MAN UTD	16	6	6	4	17	12	24
Coventry	16	6	5	5	20	21	23
Ipswich	16	4	10	2	21	19	22
Middlesbrough	16	5	6	5	26	23	21
Leeds	16	5	6	5	28	27	21
Liverpool	15	5	4	6	24	24	19
Sheff Wed.	16	4	7	5	18	19	19
Tottenham	16	4	7	5	16	22	19
Sheff Utd	16	4	5	7	16	22	17
Everton	16	4	4	8	13	20	16
Southampton	15	3	6	6	12	17	15
Oldham	16	3	6	7	23	29	15
Wimbledon	16	3	5	8	18	25	14
C. Palace	16	1	9	6	20	27	12
Nottm Forest	16	2	5	9	12	25	11

How Cantona came saw and conquered

The sky was grey and cheerless, the darkening clouds holding only the promise of another wet wintry day.

Alex Ferguson's mood as he sat at his desk deep inside Old Trafford was as sombre as the clouds that spread their gloom like a giant blanket over the city.

The faces and names of footballers who had consumed his every waking moment for the last few weeks were flickering over and over in his mind like the pages in a well-worn diary.

It was Wednesday, November 25. Ferguson was pondering his team's title chances and was beginning to wonder whether the outlook was as bleak as Manchester's inevitable weather forecast.

The fans were getting edgy, Alex Ferguson had already sensed that. What's more, he knew it was understandable. The team had just struggled through a spell of five games without a win. They were eighth in the Premier table, nine points behind the leaders Norwich.

If things did not improve fast, thoughts of the Old Trafford faithful would return to the misery at the end of the previous season when United collapsed over the last few games and virtually handed the most coveted prize in British soccer to their arch-rivals from over the Pennines, Leeds United.

That had hurt desperately on the terraces, where the supporters yearned for the return of the glory days of the Sixties. But to Ferguson, whom critics accused of cracking under the strain, it hurt more. It was like twisting a dagger in the heart of everything he had worked and dreamed for during the last seven years.

Yet Ferguson knew his team was built on solid foundations. After all, hadn't he spent endless hours nurturing the club's youth policy, encouraging home-grown talent to top up his regular dips into the transfer market?

He was delighted with the form of Peter Schmeichel, nicknamed the Terminator and a man-mountain of a goalkeeper. He was having a magnificent season, even challenging Neville Southall for the accolade of the Premier League's best goalkeeper.

He could have asked no more of his defence, where the maturing Gary Pallister and solid skipper Steve Bruce had allowed visiting strikers just 12 goals so far, the best record in the Premier League. Added to that was the guile and Trojan work-rate of chirpy Cockney Paul Ince, whose blossoming style in the absence of the injured Bryan Robson had already guaranteed him one of the first places on England manager Graham Taylor's team-sheet.

No, it was United's lack of goals that concerned Ferguson. They had recently gone four games without a goal and had scored a paltry 17 in 16 Premier matches.

Ferguson, steeped in the survival instincts of his native Glasgow, knew better than anyone that just as the law of the jungle decrees if you don't hunt long and often you don't ear, in football terms if you don't score goals freely and easily you don't win championships.

The problem had been nagging away at him for months.

He had attempted to sign England striker Alan Shearer during the summer, but could not compete with the blank cheque which Jack Walker, football's latest and richest benefactor, was prepared to hand over to Kenny Dalglish at Blackburn Rovers.

He had signed Dion Dublin from Cambridge for £1 million, only to see the striker he hoped would form a lucrative partnership with Mark Hughes break a leg after just half-a-dozen performances.

And now, with Christmas around the corner, it seemed he had played his last card with a £3.5 million bid for David Hirst of Sheffield Wednesday.

That offer hadn't only failed. It had provoked a bitter row with Wednesday manager Trevor Francis, who accused Ferguson of leaking the story to the Press to try to unsettle Hirst. Ferguson angrily denied the charges, though he did admit a signing would have taken pressure off the United Board from shareholders at that morning's annual meeting. But if he couldn't have Hirst or Shearer, who else was available? Who else could fit into Ferguson's carefully-made plans and provide the elusive final piece in the title jigsaw?

Ferguson's list, and his mind, were virtually exhausted and he was about to return to his daily chores when the office telephone rang.

Little did he know that that call ultimately held the key to breaking the jinx which had deprived Britain's most famous club of the Championship for 26 long years. Ferguson picked up the phone and heard the measured, solicitor-type tone of Martin Edwards, the Manchester United chairman, on the other end.

"Alex, I've just had Leeds' financial director Bill Fotherby on the phone. He was making enquiries about buying Denis Irwin."

"Irwin?" replied Ferguson, a little surprised. "There's no way I'd dream about even talking about selling Denis. He's been our most consistent player all season."

At which point an intriguing thought popped into Ferguson's mind. If Leeds manager Howard Wilkinson was prepared to spend more than £1 million for a top-class defender, might he not be prepared to offload a striker? After all, he was so blessed with strikers at Elland Road that he had been able to leave out his £1 million French signing Eric Cantona the previous Saturday against Arsenal.

Ferguson sat up. The adrenalin had begun to swirl through his veins. And yes, he remembered reading a newspaper report revealing that Cantona's Gallic pride had been hurt. He had flown back to France and there was a suggestion, that he was more than a little unsettled. It was worth a chance, it was certainly worth the price of a phone call.

His breath quickened, the excitement building as he spoke into the receiver. "Martin, can you phone back and ask Leeds if Cantona is available."

If Ferguson had surprised himself with the original suggestion, which he later described as "a whim, a thought completely out of the blue," he was even more shocked when Leeds came back with their reply: "When can we meet and where."

Ferguson met Cantona for the first time at the Holiday Inn in Manchester the following day.

There was no haggling, there were no snags. It was as easy as buying a bar of chocolate, though a little more expensive that your average Mars bar.

A price was fixed at £1.2 million and the Frenchman, who insists "boredom is my worst enemy," signed a three-year contract at around £4,500 a week.

The talks, ironically, were concluded in just 90 minutes, and though Ferguson was as yet unaware of the magnitude of unfolding events, he had just put together the match of the season.

The United manager told an astonished Fleet Street that night: "I was delighted when Leeds decided to accept our request. He is a very experienced player and the goal scorer we have been looking for."

Leeds manager Howard Wilkinson was also besieged by bewildered journalists searching for a supposed "real reason" why

Cantona had been let go of. Wilkinson, a man who likes to have complete control over his players in much the same mould as England manager Graham Taylor, played the straight bat for which he is renowned.

"This deal perhaps gives Eric a better chance of first team football than he would have at Leeds," said Wilkinson, who had paid £1 million to French club Nimes for the 26-year-old Marseille man the previous February. "It is impossible to pick more than 11 players. Somebody is always going to be disappointed."

HAPPY AND GLORIOUS ... Cantona, with friends, holding the French Cup after Montpelier's win in 1990. His wife Isabelle is giving the thumbs up.

It was an explanation which held as much water as a sieve with the Elland Road supporters who had afforded their favourite Frenchman cult status. Their chants of "Ooh-ah-Cantona" had been taken up far beyond the confines of Leeds, and they had been rewarded with eleven goals in 19 matches.

To the fans it didn't make sense. Why sell the one man who was ensuring the turnstiles whizzed round in a season which was rapidly becoming a battle against relegation? Why ditch the one man who was keeping the Elland Road souvenir shop in business single-handed? Above all, why sell your joint-top goal scorer? Cantona, with a hat-trick in the Charity Shield against Liverpool, and Lee Chapman had both cracked in 11 goals.

Supporters club chairman Ray Fell put the mood of the fans into sharp focus that cold November night: "My reaction to Eric's transfer is one of amazement. He had made himself a big favourite with Leeds fans. Eric has fostered a great relationship with the Elland Road crowd. Now the fans will be expecting a quick replacement."

In hindsight Wilkinson had given some hint to Cantona's fate in a book he had published, in which he had expressed nagging doubts about Cantona's ability to come to terms with the hurly burly nature of the English League game.

Nevertheless, Ferguson went to bed that night with his mind spinning. He'd landed his man, but how was he going to employ him? Would he play up front with Mark Hughes or Brian McClair? How could he reshape his side to accommodate the charismatic Frenchman, who was a great favourite of former French soccer boss Michel Platini but who also had a worrying reputation for flouting authority? He had quit French football following a sending-off for throwing the ball at the referee and insulting a disciplinary panel. At the hearing Cantona asked to be treated like any other player, but they told him: "We can't do that." It offended Cantona and when he was given a month's suspension he called them idiots. They increased the suspension to two months. Across the years in France there had also been shirt throwing and gestures to the crowd and a year's suspension from the French national side for verbally abusing their manager Henri Michel. Rumours also told of fierce arguments in dressing rooms.

Indeed, Cantona had first come to England to escape all that. Platini, acting on behalf of his favourite player, rang Trevor Francis at Sheffield Wednesday and asked him to give the colourful Frenchman a trial. Platini pleaded: "He sees things quicker than the others, he understands quicker. He's an intelligent type of man." Francis, who had not seen Cantona play, agreed to the trial in January 1992. Cantona went to Hillsborough on a bitingly cold morning. There was a film of frost across the training ground and Cantona had to prove everything to Francis on Astroturf. Francis, undecided, asked if the trial could be extended by a further week. Cantona's reply was in French but Francis got the message: "Au revoir." The headlines screamed "Brat walks out on Trev," "Frog legs it home" and "Francis in fury as moaner Cantona quits." It was the first direct example of the tempestuous Gallic temperament in action in England.

One way or another the sparks were going to fly during the next few months at Old Trafford.

The next day Ferguson curled his Glaswegian tongue around a smattering of schoolboy French and introduced his new signing to an excited gathering of the world's Press with the words "Mon plaisir presenter Eric Cantona."

The questions from a packed hall were English and blunt. Had he asked Leeds for a transfer? At the same time the Leeds United switchboard 45 miles away was being swamped by calls from irate supporters demanding refunds on their season tickets.

Eric Cantona, however, insisted through his interpreter in quiet, clipped, urgent French: "My working relationship with Leeds didn't break down. My few months there were among the best I've ever had in the game from the point of view of the manager, players and fans.

"It might seem unthinkable to some people at Leeds for me to come to Manchester United, but I see it as a positive move.

"I can understand that some Leeds fans may feel I have let them down. But in no way do I feel that. I hope I have reached my spiritual home."

Cantona hoped he had set the record straight. Little did he reckon with the tenacity of the soccer Press and its ability to keep a juicy pot boiling.

Rumour and counter-rumour surfaced, the wilder reports even suggesting Cantona had stormed out of Elland Road after being left out of the home game with Arsenal. Other unsubstantiated gossip sweeping the terraces hinted at problems with Leeds team-mates.

The story which has stood the test of time is by no means the most intriguing. It is simply that Howard Wilkinson believed Cantona could not perform the job he wanted him to do for Leeds away from Elland Road. But perhaps he was also influenced by the eccentricities and fluctuating moods for which the Frenchman is famed. Whatever, it could turn out to be the biggest professional clanger of Wilkinson's career.

The simmering row rumbled on into the next week when Cantona flew to Portugal, where he was to make his United debut in Lisbon's Stadium of Light – the ground a young, inspired George Best lit up with a blazing two-goal performance in United's famous 5-1 European Cup quarter-final victory in 1966.

This latest match between United and Benfica was to celebrate Eusebio's 50th birthday and the 25th anniversary of United's 1968 European Cup triumph at Wembley.

It was in danger of being overshadowed by the continuing feud between Leeds and Cantona until Alex Ferguson stepped in on the eve of the game, telling reporters: "We're not even thinking about all the innuendo about Eric – this man can become a giant at Old Trafford.

"All that matters is what happens on the pitch. A lot of card marking has been going on about Eric and I understand that. But we don't need to get involved.

"Let Eric enjoy playing for Manchester United – everyone does that – and all the peripheral things about off-field problems won't matter. I'm not looking for confrontations, he's now a United player. The business is done."

With that Cantona prepared for the business of actually playing for Manchester United in front of 50,000 fans.

Ferguson's plan was to give Cantona two 45-minute work-outs, playing first alongside Brian McClair and then Mark Hughes, the idea being to gauge his best strike partnership for the following Sunday's Manchester derby.

And though Cantona didn't score on his Manchester debut he showed enough close control, vision and coolness under pressure to convince his new boss that the gamble he'd taken following that fateful phone call just six days before was a winner.

He might have nicked a debut goal if Brazilian defender William hadn't blocked a shot with his shins just before half-time.

Benfica just about deserved to win what was a low-key match with a goal from 20-year-old Rui Costa nine minutes from time.

The one sour note which left just a tinge of apprehension with Ferguson as he caught the night-flight home was a booking for his new signing – punishment for a fierce tackle on Benfica substitute Abel. At least that threw doubt on any implication that Cantona didn't do his fair share of tackling.

Cantona's League debut came the following Sunday when he was brought on as substitute for Ryan Giggs in the Manchester derby which United won 2-1 with goals from Paul Ince and Mark Hughes. And then it happened. The great sleeping giant that was United stirred from the slumber which had brought just six goals in seven games. And, once awake, there was a new alertness. A fresh vigour in the work of Hughes and McClair, a new intelligence to the running of Lee Sharpe and an added breathtaking dimension to the finishing of Giggs.

It was as if Cantona's arrival had lit a fire which could not be extinguished. It raged for the next seven games in which United blasted 18 goals, with Cantona scoring in four consecutive League matches. Suddenly, where there had been anxiety and indecision there was confidence and freedom. The team conspired almost overnight to find a common glorious, exhilarating purpose with Cantona providing the vision, the deft touches and, above all, the subtle routes to goal which allowed United to become, not just the most effective football side in the Premier League, but also by far the most exciting.

At last, here was a team to bring style, panache and raw, gut-wrenching thrills back to the Theatre of Dreams. The critics, and there were many who had poured scorn on Ferguson's decision to buy Cantona, were forced to start eating their words. They included George Best, who still regularly visits Old Trafford, and who admitted after one resounding 4-1 victory over Spurs: "I didn't think Cantona would fit in here. But today he has convinced me that at £1.2 million he is the shrewdest buy Alex Ferguson has made since he came here. That was the most stylish performance I have seen from United for some time."

It is a tribute to Cantona's unique qualities that one man could trigger such a striking metamorphosis. But then the swarthy Cantona, at 6ft 3ins and with the gait of a guardsman, is not your average soccer player plucked from the back streets of a working-class community or reared in some antiseptic comprehensive in English suburbia.

In Cantona there lurks an indefinable quality, something akin to the gipsy. It breeds a constant search for adventure, a nomad's eye for a new challenge. It has seen him change clubs ten times already and, at 26, he is still at least a couple of years from his sporting peak. He is a man with no regrets, he never looks back.

He possesses that devil-may-care spontaneity which you might expect from someone born in Paris and raised among the more Latin quarters of the South of France. He is a poet, a philosopher and a musician – he plays the piano. He spends quiet hours at an easel painting and his beautiful wife of five years, Isabelle, describes his vivid works as sometimes "passionate" sometimes "pretty" according to his mood. She also maintains he is much misunderstood. "I can't believe they call him aggresive," she says. "If they saw him with his son they wouldn't say that, or when he's playing with the dog. He's a fantastic father and he's very good company, very pleasant and very generous with his time – completely different to how people see him. At home he's absolutely adorable. He's fantastic around the house, so calm and relaxed. I might scream a bit but he just shrugs and says 'It doesn't matter' no matter what it is."

FRENCH IMPRESSIONIST
… Eric Cantona takes great pride in his painting.

Others however, sometimes paint him as arrogant and aloof. Yet when talking about his contribution to the title triumph he has been remarkably generous to those around him. Almost to the point of modesty. "People draw attention to me," he says. "But it is the personality of the team that is important. If I had wanted to draw attention to myself I would have become a singles tennis player. Or found a nice little girl to play mixed doubles with. We started to score goals but that is why they bought me. I came here to make the difference. The style of play suits me. They have marvellous players here. The most important thing is the collective, for this is a team game."

But wherever Cantona goes it seems he is destined to be the centre of attention, the one who is singled out for high praise or scathing criticism. There is no middle ground with Cantona. It was inevitable that all eyes would be on him alone when he returned for the first time with United to Elland Road on a sharp Monday night in February. But Cantona could not have been prepared for the reception committee waiting for him. He was virtually ambushed as he clambered off the United coach in the Elland Road car park by a milling throng of Leeds supporters whose venom was as loud as it was abhorrent.

The dressing rooms were close but Cantona must have felt like a man on his way to the guillotine. He can never have taken a more intimidating walk as he pushed through the same people who had taken him to their hearts the autumn before. Outwardly Cantona dismissed it without as much as a Gallic shrug but not even he could have been unaffected by such an intense demonstration of animosity.

It was no surprise when he twice squandered excellent opportunities which would have given United a three-point lead in the Premier League. He also collected a yellow card for a niggling clash with Jon Newsome. The match was a thrilling contest even though it ended goalless. But as Cantona strode off the pitch he careered headlong into fresh controversy. As he neared the touchline the crowd aimed one last blast of vitriol at their former idol. They screeched "scum," "traitor," and worse and Cantona broke into a trot to reach the sanctuary of the player's tunnel. It seemed his ordeal was over. In fact, it had just begun.

As he changed, police officers arrived outside the United dressing rooms. They wanted to interview Cantona, saying Leeds fans had accused him of spitting at them as he left the field. The West Yorkshire police decided to take no further action but one fan, Mark Edwards, a businessman from Haverfordwest, was not satisfied. He claimed he was hit in the face by Cantona's spittle and he complained to the FA.

His allegation was supported by a written statement from a policeman who said he had witnessed the incident. The FA charged Cantona with misconduct and it seemed he was certain to get the same punishment as Arsenal's Ian Wright who was fined £1,500 for spitting at Oldham fans in November 1991. In face, the disciplinary hearing took into consideration the provocation Cantona had suffered at Elland Road and he was fined £1,000 and warned about his future conduct.

Mr Edwards felt vindicated, saying: "I'm glad the truth is out, people kept asking me if I had made it up. But there were a lot of witnesses. They saw what happened. Everybody loved him at Leeds. He was under pressure when he came back, but there was no excuse for what happened. But, even so, I still think he is one of the best players in the League. I only wanted an apology." Cantona sought no such expressions of regret from the thousands who had wished him harm that torrid night.

With the incident closed and after a two-match ban for totting up 21 points, which kept him out of games at Liverpool and Oldham, Cantona returned to the action and the goals flowed once more like fine red wine.

When Ferguson finally wrapped his arms around the Premier League trophy in the drama of May it was United's first title in 26 years. For Cantona, the man who makes things happen, it was his second Championship in successive seasons. "He has brought something extra that we haven't had since I came here," said Ferguson. "He is capable of producing things with his vision and touch. It's wonderful. A lot of players have come to this club and found it too much for them. He's lifted everyone round about him."

As the celebrations ensued in the post-title days of euphoria, Cantona seemed content with life. He was happy in his modest, semi-detached home in a quiet suburb of Leeds. His wife was enjoying her job lecturing in French at Leeds University. Their four-year-old son, Raphael, was settling into school. Cantona, on one hour-long trip back across the Moors to Yorkshire, observed, it is said, that "this is good shooting and fishing country." Maybe Cantona was thinking of settling down to the good life, taking things easy for a change. Maybe. But no one, least of all Alex Ferguson, was betting on that!

PEDIGREE CHUMS ... Cantona walking out with his favrourite pets.

November 28

United celebrated the start of a new era, a new year almost and it was a case of in with the new … and in with the old.

As Eric Cantona sat in the directors' box at Highbury, regally waving to the battery of lenses aimed at him, out on the pitch, United's old guard was making its own statement.

Bryan Robson, Captain Marvel of yore, was once again guiding the good ship United, the number seven on his back like a beacon, a symbol that when Robbo's about, all is well. "Steady as she goes. Watch out for boarders."

Robson gave United the contribution they had needed all season, strengthening the defence, holding the midfield together and setting free the forward line.

While Monsieur Eric, his crewcut-framed face, smiling pixie-like at anyone who turned his way, lapped up the starlight like an Oscar winner arriving at a preview, our Bryan was out there proving that good old English midfielders are the stuff footballing epics are made of. Instead of Ooh La La, make the script Howay the Lad.

ARSENAL 0

MANCHESTER UNITED 1

(Half-time score: 0-1)

Arsenal: Seaman, Dixon, Adams, Bould, Morrow, Jensen (Parlour 65), Hillier, Merson, Campbell, Wright, Limpar (Flatts 85).
Sub: Miller
Booked: Adams
United: Schmeichel, Parker, Bruce, Pallister, Irwin, Giggs, Robson, Ince, Sharpe, Hughes, McClair. Subs: Phelan, Kanchelskis, Digby
Scorer: Hughes 27
Booked: Hughes
Referee: H King (Merthyr Tydfil)
Attendance: 29,739
Weather: Cold

Hi! Eric Cantona watches his new team-mates beat Arsenal.

Cantona's signing would prove to be Alex Ferguson's master stroke in the campaign for that elusive championship. But who is to say but United might have wrapped up the title earlier had they had a fit Robson all season.

His presence here was enough as United won big on the big stage for the first time since the early part of the season.

Cantona, without lacing a boot or tugging on a jersey, certainly seemed to galvanise United's forwards Mark Hughes and Brian McClair. It was felt that they might be the ones under threat from the arrival of the big Frenchman with the ramrod-straight back and the football touch of an angel.

And there was even a case made for keeping Cantona in his cushioned seat if the effect was to spark United into a performance such as this.

As Ferguson said: "Eric will have seen today how difficult it is going to be to get into the side. What I have tried to do is bring an international player to our club and create a competitive edge up front.

"Maybe when Dion Dublin got his bad break I should have gone and bought then, right away, and kept that edge going within the club."

But what pleased him just as much was the balance and shape brought to the side by Robson, making only his fourth start of the season. The sorcerer, playing with his apprentice Paul Ince alongside, cast an influence over the midfield that mesmerised Arsenal's duo of David Hillier and John Jensen.

Ferguson added: "The balance is far, far better with Robson because I can play two strikers through the middle. People might scratch their head when I say that, but when Bryan is there he is able to shape players around him.

"Ince and Darren (Ferguson, the manager's son) don't have the experience to exercise that control, so if we played with two men wide we tended to be exposed. To counter that we have been pulling Brian McClair back to give us extra strength in midfield and he has suffered through that.

"Hopefully Bryan can keep fit. But how many times have I said that before…?"

Tony Adams, once tipped as Robson's replacement as captain of England, was unstinting in his appraisal of Robson. "He's a magnificent player," said the Arsenal central defender. "I was fortunate to play under him at international level and he's a fabulous skipper and a fabulous player."

Robson it was who frustrated the Arsenal threat from Paul Merson, while young Ryan Giggs, on the eve of his 19th birthday, wove his magic on the right flank. Added Ferguson: "The boy has the talent to play anywhere. We try to keep him as free as we can to allow him to do what he is good at, beating men."

Following his strike at Oldham, Hughes again got on the scoresheet while McClair seemed to enjoy his move back up front.

It left Ferguson with a poser for the forthcoming derby crunch with Manchester City. Does he play Cantona? Will he fit in? "I don't know," said Fergie affording himself a winner's smile. "Right now, I'm panicking…"

Mais oui? NON!

League Table After Match

	P	W	D	L	F	A	Pts
Norwich	17	11	3	3	32	30	36
Blackburn	17	8	7	2	26	12	31
Arsenal	17	9	2	6	22	17	29
Aston Villa	17	7	7	3	26	18	28
MAN UTD	17	7	6	4	18	12	27
QPR	17	7	5	5	22	17	26
Man City	17	7	4	6	24	17	25
Liverpool	17	7	4	6	30	24	25
Chelsea	16	7	4	5	23	19	25
Ipswich	17	5	10	2	22	19	25
Coventry	17	6	6	5	21	22	24
Tottenham	17	5	7	5	17	22	22
Leeds	16	5	6	5	28	27	21
Middlesbrough	17	5	6	6	27	27	21
Sheff Wed	17	4	8	5	19	20	20
Southampton	17	4	7	6	15	19	19
Oldham	17	4	6	7	27	30	18
Sheff Utd	17	4	6	7	17	23	18
Everton	17	4	4	9	13	21	16
Wimbledon	17	3	6	8	19	26	15
C Palace	17	1	9	7	20	32	12
Nottm Forest	17	2	5	10	13	27	11

December 6

If there had ever been any doubts that Mark Hughes could carry United's attack to the title, then an explosive derby performance answered them.

Hughes, Welsh-born but made for Manchester, won an emotive match and spelled out that not even £1.2 million Eric Cantona would dislodge him.

When Ron Atkinson's United won ten straight victories in 1985 and looked like a championship banker, many blamed Hughes for the subsequent slump. Once his end of season move to Spanish aristos Barcelona was signed and sealed, Hughes' form understandably nosedived as he awaited his final call-up overseas.

But his move back to Old Trafford in 1988 for £1.5 million was greeted like the return of the prodigal and Hughes, muscular, aggressive and willing to give his all for the United cause, ensured he would always be a favourite son of the Stretford End.

And all this season, as he battled alone up front, the fans refused to blame our Sparky. With his ultimately winning strike here, his third goal in as many games and ninth of the season, Highes began to repay the faith of the faithful; and his manager Alex Ferguson.

Said Ferguson: "Sparky has been scoring regularly all season. It was his ninth today and he could easily be heading for the best tally of his career."

Arms spread wide, this consummate showman milked the rich applause that cascaded around Old Trafford like the Manchester rain that wept buckets on this 117th derby.

But Hughes insisted: "The winner I got against Arsenal last week probably gave me just as much pleasure. I'm reasonably happy with my performance and hopefully the goals will continue to come. Eric Cantona is a very good player.

"I wouldn't say his signing had resulted in any more effort from the strikers at Old Trafford – you have to play for United at full revs every week anyway."

Although Niall Quinn, sweeping up following a collision between United skipper Steve Bruce and keeper Peter Schmeichel, pulled a goal back for City within 60 seconds of Hughes' 75th minute thunderbolt, no one could deny a resurgent United the points.

But they had to be earned the hard way and nowhere more than in the heart of midfield where this rawest of derbies was decided. When you have Bryan Robson, Paul Ince, Steve McMahon and subsequently Peter Reid in close proximity, you light the blue touchpaper and stand back.

It was fierce and frenetic but Ince rose above it all majestically, riding the sledgehammer tackles of McMahon to emerge the victor in the battle.

Ince, the Cockney Kid who wanted to move to Old Trafford so much he even posed in a United shirt before any deal was done, has grown up this season. United – and England – owe him a huge debt.

Robson, from whose shadow Ince has stunningly emerged, fired the first shot in this latest battle in the age old campaign between the two Manchester rivals, to test City goalkeeper Tony Coton.

But the opening goal was an explosive as the match itself. Hughes turned Robson's 20th minute free kick into the area and Bruce laid it back to Ince who shot inside the post with fearsome power.

The Manchester version of British Bulldog continued in midfield and City's Ricl Holden was booked as referee Gerald Ashby moved quickly to exercise firm control.

Ryan Giggs tantalised City and he enabled Denis Irwin to whip a ball across Coton's goal, the keeper just touching it out with his fingers. Despite the commitment of Holden and the aerial threat of Quinn, City were always marginally second best, but Fitzroy Simpson should have equalised just before half-time when he shot just wide.

The restart saw the arrival of Cantona for his United debut, a generous reception from the fans and a not so generous one from McMahon. The Frenchman responded with a couple of lovely crosses, the second of which Hughes ought to have converted, but as Ferguson said later: "Anyone coming into a derby finds it hard. Eric still showed some great touches and two or three great crosses, but he will be glad to get that one over."

The midfield maelstrom was given an added dimension with the arrival of City player-boss Reid. The former England man, all bustle and muscle and economical stride, sparked City and as if in response, McMahon was at last booked for one tackle too many on Ince.

But the game looked won for United when Hughes controlled the ball on his chest 25 yards out, collected a rebound off Curle, and hammered a perfect dipping shot past Coton. However, United fans were still celebrating when Holden broke clear, crossed and in the mix-up between Schmeichel and Bruce, Quinn stabbed the ball home.

*MAN-IN-WAITING …
Cantona moments before making his debut.*

League Table After Match

	P	W	D	L	F	A	Pts
Norwich	18	12	3	3	34	31	39
Blackburn	18	8	7	3	28	15	31
Aston Villa	18	8	7	3	28	19	31
Chelsea	18	9	4	5	26	20	31
MAN UTD	18	8	6	4	20	13	30
QPR	18	8	5	5	25	19	29
Arsenal	18	9	2	7	22	19	29
Ipswich	18	5	11	2	24	21	26
Liverpool	17	7	4	6	30	24	25
Man City	18	7	4	7	25	19	25
Coventry	18	6	7	5	23	24	25
Middlesbrough	18	6	6	6	30	29	24
Southampton	18	5	7	6	17	19	22
Tottenham	18	5	7	6	18	24	22
Leeds	18	5	6	7	29	32	21
Sheff Wed	18	4	8	6	20	22	20
Oldham	18	4	6	8	29	33	18
Sheff Utd	18	4	6	8	17	25	18
Everton	17	4	4	9	13	21	16
Wimbledon	18	3	6	9	20	28	15
C Palace	18	2	9	7	22	32	15
Nottm Forest	18	3	5	10	17	28	14

*ARMS AND THE MAN …
Hughes' joy after scoring
against City.*

Schmeichel then had to make a fine double save from Andy Hill and David White and Ferguson admitted: "I had just started to relax when City pulled one back and we needed Schmeichel to keep us in it.

"But we were very pleased with a third win in a row. We know our fans will regard it as a fantastic result and we don't want to let Norwich force too much daylight between us at the top of the table."

Norwich, though, United's next opponents, would soon learn that United were fast putting out the lights on the rest of the Premier League.

December 12

They had conceded four at Anfield to Liverpool, three to Manchester City at Main Road and seven at Blackburn Rovers – hardly the most impressive credentials for a championship chasing side. But Norwich City had manfully built an eight-point advantage at the top of the table. They were the surprise team of the season, a club without stars, a graveyard for players who did not quite make it elsewhere.

Three of their back four had been imported from Tottenham Hotspur, where they were regarded as having more mongrel than pedigree. This was a game United had to win. Even at this rather early stage of the campaign Alex Ferguson could not contemplate clawing back 12 points. For him, the pressure was beginning to build.

He said: "When Manchester United suffer a defeat it is regarded as a crisis. That is the reminder that winning is the only thing which matters here. All the time victory is demanded – and because we get so much attention the way we play is so important."

In contrast, Fergie's Norwich counterpart Mike Walker had already exceeded all expectations. United strove desperately in search of the Holy Grail while Walker had his eye on making sure his side would avoid relegation as soon as possible. He admitted: "When you start the season as relegation favourites like we did then you have to do that."

Norwich had flourished on the backs of their excellent home form but an afternoon in the Theatre of Dreams was to prove a rude awakening for the colourful Canaries. United took three priceless points thanks to a single goal, punishing an error from one of Norwich's best players, Daryl Sutch, offering the jubilant Mark Hughes an opportunist's chance he gratefully gobbled up.

Yet so much of what went on before and after the crucial goal had a touch of sophistication with Eric Cantona, as ever, adding nice touches, which were not lost on Ferguson. "His first pass was only six yards but it opened up the whole game. He does simple things like that," said Fergie. United had delivered the goods – just. The view that Norwich are an average team playing average football, occupying an above average position, appeared more than a mite unkind.

MANCHESTER UNITED 1

NORWICH 0

(Half-time score: 0-0)

United: Schmeichel, Parker, Bruce, Pallister, Irwin, Sharpe, Ince, McClair, Giggs, Cantona, Hughes. Subs: Digby, Kanchelskis, Blackmore
Scorer: Hughes 59
Norwich: Gunn, Culverhouse, Polston, Butterworth, Bowen, Fox, Sutch, Crook (Megson 16), Phillips, Beckford (Sutton 75), Robins. Sub: Marshall
Referee: R Milford (Bristol)
Attendance: 34,500
Weather: Fine

Norwich keeper Bryan Gunn saves from Cantona.

Few fancied them to stay the distance and that number was further diminished. Today, Fergie's great expectations had been met and he lavished praise on the visitors. "You respect them as they are the team that has shown championship form. They like to play football and stick to their principles."

True, the warm applause which accompanied their departure from the Old Trafford arena acclaimed the fact that they had brought some bright sunshine into the Premier League. But there was another low fast approaching East Anglia.

"We are going to have setbacks, it is how you react to them that matters. We have had a couple and responded well," said Walker. Norwich's next stop was a tricky skirmish with Ipswich at Carrow Roads. United looked ahead knowing a semblance of reality could soon be brought to the top of the Premier League.

League Table After Match

	P	W	D	L	F	A	Pts
Norwich	19	12	3	4	34	32	39
Aston Villa	19	9	7	3	30	20	34
MAN UTD	19	9	6	4	21	13	33
Chelsea	19	9	5	5	26	20	32
Blackburn	18	8	7	3	28	15	31
Ipswich	19	6	11	2	27	22	29
QPR	19	8	5	6	26	22	29
Arsenal	19	9	2	8	22	20	29
Coventry	19	6	8	5	25	26	26
Liverpool	18	7	4	7	31	26	25
Man City	19	7	4	8	26	22	25
Middlesbrough	19	6	7	6	30	29	25
Southampton	19	5	8	6	19	21	23
Tottenham	19	6	7	6	19	24	25
Leeds	19	6	6	7	32	33	24
Sheff Wed	19	4	8	7	21	25	20
Oldham	19	4	6	9	31	38	18
Sheff Utd	19	5	6	8	18	25	21
Everton	19	5	4	10	15	23	19
Wimbledon	19	4	6	9	25	30	18
C Palace	19	3	9	7	25	33	18
Nottm Forest	19	3	5	11	18	30	14

December 19

United were on a tremendous roll, the home victory over Norwich City the previous Saturday was their fourth on the trot, but still there was much ground to be made up.

Chelsea, just a point adrift of United in fifth place, offered formidable opposition on their own patch. They, too, at the time, had genuine League title aspirations and gave very little away. The match, played on a damp, dreary wet December afternoon, started tediously and went further downhill

It desperately needed the kiss of life, but unfortunately for United the resuscitation was done by Chelsea's defender David Lee. It was a lead the Blues had marginally deserved but it wasn't to last. The game had entered the final furlong when a young colt by the

CHELSEA 1

MANCHESTER UNITED 1

(Half-time score: 0-0)

Chelsea: Hitchcock, Hall, Sinclair, Lee, Donaghy, Stuart, Wise, Townsend, Newton, Le Saux, Fleck (Harford 66). Subs: Burley, Colgan
Scorer: Lee 67
Booked: Fleck
United: Schmeichel, Parker, Pallister, Bruce, Irwin, Phelan (Kanchelskis 83), Ince, McClair, Sharpe, Hughes, Cantona. Subs: Blackmore, Digby
Scorer: Cantona 71
Booked: Pallister, Hughes
Referee: R Lewis (Gt Bookham)
Attendance: 34,464
Weather: Wet

TOUCH OF CLASS …
Cantona shows his skill.

name of Lee Sharpe sprinted clear to create an equaliser for, who else, but the charismatic Eric Cantona.

Two points dropped … but Alex Ferguson was quick to point to a bonus, the restoration of Lee Sharpe as one of football's radiant talents. It has been a long furlough for a boy who made his breakthrough at 19 then had a deep groin injury followed by persistent meningitis.

"Lee's emergence has been a real bonus for me. You just don't expect that kind of illness to strike a young footballer," said Fergie. "Lee has acquitted himself magnificently and it is a relief to have him back in the side. His great asset is his wonderful temperament. He is not a flatterer. He is a deliverer. He can produce the killing crosses like that one today and he can finish, too."

It is Fergie's theory that two years having to watch the game from the stands have improved Sharpe's understanding and perception of the game. He added:"For two years he was able to watch and his knowledge of the game has surprised me. Young English players don't see that many matches any more because they are always playing. Some of them don't have the passion they might have if they had been standing on the terraces. I never stopped watching as a kid."

Sharpe believes his own gathering maturity has also made him more aware that the game is not just about beating your full back. He says: "There were times when I thought it might be difficult to get back into the side. I got the meningitis just two days into pre-season training. Every time I tried to do anything energetic I found myself back in hospital."

Since his return Sharpe has displayed the form which indicates that the torment and uncertainty are at last a thing of the past, barely a bad memory. And unlike teammates Ryan Giggs and Andrei Kanchelskis, there is a certain directness about Sharpe's contribution.

He says:"When I get the ball in a crossing position I'm not fussy about beating the defender. The extra strength I have now means I don't need as much space to run on to the ball to cross it."

Ferguson has no doubts that Sharpe is now a much, much better player than he was when he won his first international cap in March 1991. Another England call wasn't to be far away, but for now Sharpe's improvement by the match was just the tonic United were looking for. Tough matches at Sheffield Wednesday and at home to Coventry were looming over the crucial Christmas period.

All Sharpe really needed to complete his rehabilitation was a goal!

League Table After Match

	P	W	D	L	F	A	Pts
Norwich	19	12	3	4	34	22	36
Aston Villa	20	9	8	3	31	21	35
Blackburn	20	9	7	4	30	17	34
MAN UTD	20	9	7	4	22	14	34
Chelsea	20	9	6	5	27	21	33
Arsenal	20	9	3	8	23	21	30
Ipswich	19	6	11	2	27	22	29
Coventry	20	7	8	5	30	27	29
QPR	20	8	5	7	26	23	29
Liverpool	20	8	4	8	34	32	28
Man City	20	7	5	8	27	23	26
Middlesbrough	20	6	8	6	31	30	26
Tottenham	20	6	7	7	20	26	25
Leeds	19	6	6	7	32	33	24
Sheff Wed	20	5	8	7	22	25	23
Southampton	20	5	8	7	20	23	23
Everton	20	6	4	10	17	24	22
Oldham	20	5	6	9	33	39	21
Sheff Utd	20	5	6	9	18	26	21
Wimbledon	19	4	6	9	25	30	18
C Palace	19	3	9	7	25	33	18
Nottm Forest	19	3	5	11	18	30	14

December 26

By early afternoon on Boxing Day, the road to the summit was looking rockier than ever. Hillsborough, a fine stadium, has witnessed moments of joy and few will ever forget the tragedy which killed 96 people. Today, it was about to host an extraordinary occasion, a match many would store in their memory banks to relate to their grandchildren.

Sheffield Wednesday were in the midst of a mediocre campaign and languished a massive 16 points behind the leaders Norwich. Later, of course, they were to grace the Wembley stage in both the FA and Coca Cola Cup finals. United's fanatical hordes were early to rise and headed in expectation across the snow capped peaks of the Pennines. The tranquillity was about to be shattered by a game of supreme quality, excitement and the unexpected.

For many thousands of other soccer fans driving to see their own favourites at the conventional 3pm kick-off time, the breathtaking action that crackled from their car radios possibly eclipsed anything they were to witness later. It couldn't have gone more wrong for United in a frantic opening hour. Incredibly, the bubble was about to burst good and proper as Wednesday turned on an awesome display of attacking power to clock up what seemed to be an unassailable lead.

United had wanted so much to relieve ambitious Wednesday of their £3.5m rated England international David Hirst. Owls boss Trevor Francis was angry about United's interest in the player and sent out Hirst to do what he does best – and he hit United inside three minutes. Five league games without a goal had stung Hirst into action. He got the first and his superbly judged headed passes across the box set up further goals for Mark Bright and Irish midfielder John Sheridan. Three-nil down, half an hour to go, surely there was to be no way back for Fergie's fighters.

Lee Sharpe, now completely revived and with lavish praise from his manager still ringing in his ears from that outstanding display at Chelsea, had other ideas. His wretched season was about to take another turn for the better in a pulsating finale. Sharpe, once again showing excellent qualities on the left-hand side of the field, dismantled shell-shocked Wednesday with his pace and pin-point

SHEFFIELD WEDNESDAY 3

MANCHESTER UNITED 3

(Half-time score: 2-0)

Wednesday: Woods, Nilsson, Anderson, Shirtliff, Worthington, Waddle, Sheridan, Palmer, Wilson (Harkes 73), Bright, Hirst. Subs: Williams, Pressman
Scorers: Hirst 2, Bright 6, Sheridan 62
Booked: Bright
United: Schmeichel, Parker, Bruce, Pallister, Irwin, Giggs (Kanchelskis 68), Ince, McClair, Sharpe, Cantona, Hughes. Subs: Phelan, Digby
Scorers: McClair 67, 80, Cantona 84
Booked: Bruce, Hughes
Referee: A Buksh (London)
Attendance: 37,708
Weather: Cold

crosses. Twenty-nine minutes to go and Brian McClair, breaking from mid-field, fired in United's first. A consolation perhaps? Minutes later the writing was on the wall as the Scottish international took advantage of some appalling defending to add a second.

Now United were rampant, the Leppings Lane, a sea of red and white, was roaring its approval, the decibel count had increased tenfold. United were in the salvage business. Wednesday boss Francis could not really believe the score when his side went three-up – what was to follow was to take even more digesting. Ryan Giggs, looking pale and out of sorts on his return from injury, had left the arena to be replaced by Andrei Kanchelskis. Different personnel but United's determination remained undiminished.

Ferguson's gamble sparked United's Last Hurrah. No question, this was to be a point gained rather than lost. And inevitably, minutes from time justice was done. Eric Cantona may be a devotee of the beautiful game but he is still ready to scratch and scrape for goals. The Frenchman has scored some classics in his time but few less crafted than the equaliser he scuffed in at the second attempt. The celebrations were long and loud but Cantona was taking it all in his gallic stride.

He said:"I think I showed I can score from close range opportunities as well as the more spectacular efforts. Goals like that are just as important as the beautiful ones that perhaps I am better known for. I feel I can fill any role Manchester United want from me whether it's a playmaker or defender or finishing off chances. It all comes easy to me. I'm sure that goal delighted our fans." He wasn't far wrong.

League Table After Match

	P	W	D	L	F	A	Pts
Norwich	21	12	4	5	34	34	40
Blackburn	21	10	7	4	33	18	37
MAN UTD	21	9	8	4	25	17	35
Aston Villa	21	9	8	4	31	24	35
Chelsea	21	9	7	5	28	22	34
Ipswich	21	7	12	2	29	22	33
Coventry	21	8	8	5	33	27	32
Arsenal	21	9	4	8	23	21	31
Man City	21	8	5	8	29	23	29
QPR	20	8	5	7	26	23	29
Liverpool	20	8	4	8	34	32	28
Middlesbrough	21	6	9	6	33	32	27
Tottenham	21	6	8	7	20	26	26
Sheff Wed	21	5	9	7	25	28	24
Southampton	21	5	9	7	21	24	24
Leeds	21	6	6	9	33	37	24
C Palace	21	5	9	7	28	33	24
Everton	21	6	5	10	19	26	23
Oldham	20	5	6	9	33	39	21
Sheff Utd	21	5	6	10	18	24	21
Wimbledon	21	4	7	10	26	33	19
Nottm Forest	20	3	6	11	19	31	15

United players celebrate with the crowd after Cantona's goal.

December 28

If the action at Hillsborough on Boxing Day was white hot, United amazingly were about to raise the temperature even further at the Premier League summit.

Coventry City, FA Cup winners in the 80s but for so long considered whipping boys for the cream in the top flight, were enjoying a renaissance under the dynamic management of Bobby Gould and Phil Neal.

Astonishingly, they arrived at Old Trafford with a spring in their step on the backs of a sensational double success. They made a talented Aston Villa outfit look more like chumps than prospective champs and went on to hammer five goals past an ailing Liverpool side at Highfield.

MANCHESTER UNITED 5

COVENTRY 0

(Half-time score: 2-0)

United: Schmeichel, Parker, Irwin, Bruce (Phelan 59), Sharpe, Pallister, Cantona, Ince, McClair, Hughes, Giggs (Kanchelskis 79). Sub: Digby
Scorers: Giggs 6, Hughes 40, Cantona 64 (pen), Sharpe 78, Irwin 83
Coventry: Gould, Borrows, Babb, Atherton, Sansom, Williams (Ndlovu 45), McGrath, Hurst, Rosario, Quinn, Gallacher. Subs: Pearce, Ogrizovic
Booked: McGrath
Referee: R Groves (Weston-Super-Mare)
Attendance: 36,025
Weather: Cold but fine

Giggs salutes his opener while Parker and Cantona join in.

They also paraded Mick Quinn, a catalyst in their recent revival, a bustling Liverpudlian who had taken the League by storm with his considerable goal-scoring prowess. Quinn had his sights set firmly on shooting down United – but as it turned out he didn't get a kick all afternoon.

Coventry boss Gould opted to play his son Jonathan in goal … then sat back and watched him beaten five times as rampant United steamrollered their way to within three points of the top.

Six minutes gone and the reds were on the march. Ryan Giggs, substituted during the Sheffield Wednesday epic five days earlier, must have feared losing his place. Press talk of him being coveted by AC Milan and other top European clubs had contrived to take the sparkle off the shining star.

His response was magnificent and truly emphatic. Lloyd McGrath's headed clearance out of the box found Giggs lurking in space and he shaped instantly for a cross.

Quickly he eyed an opening and bent a left foot drive across the face of the box and the ball clattered in off young Gould's right-hand post. It was the perfect start to an afternoon of attacking craft that completely destroyed the visitors.

Mark Hughes, Denis Irwin, a penalty from the inspirational Eric Cantona, and Lee Sharpe gave United the win they deserved. Sharpe's strike was a mis-hit which luckily found the target but it finally represented another massive change of luck for the big-hearted youngster.

No wonder he celebrated it in style. Dogged by injuries and horrendous illness, his season was at last about to move into overdrive. He admitted:"I've been desperate to score in the last few games and that will ease me a bit. I don't think I've ever played in a better team performance than that. It makes things so much easier for me, the lads are really pleased with their efforts today."

Alex Ferguson was overjoyed with his side's super five star show. "It was a fantastic performance especially after the Sheffield Wednesday draw. We must have made 30 chances in the two games. Coventry had scored five against Liverpool, slaughtered Villa and we couldn't have met them at a worse time.

Bobby Gould, graceful in defeat, admitted: "I reckon we're six years and £60m behind United. My players had the pedestal kicked from under their feet by a barrage of attacking."

But as he left a deserted Old Trafford, Gould issued words of caution. "Remember, United beat Oldham 6-3 at Christmas last year and faltered late on … but they will have learned from that lesson and won't go overboard about this one."

Never a truer word was spoken ... only time would tell.

Left: SHARP SHOOTER ...
Lee Sharpe slams in the fourth.

Below: TAKE FIVE ...
Denis Irwin cracks the fifth
against Coventry.

League Table After Match

	P	W	D	L	F	A	Pts
Norwich	22	12	5	5	34	34	41
MAN UTD	22	10	8	4	30	17	38
Aston Villa	22	10	8	4	32	24	38
Blackburn	22	10	7	5	34	20	37
Ipswich	22	8	12	2	31	23	36
Chelsea	22	9	8	5	28	22	35
QPR	21	9	5	7	30	25	32
Coventry	22	8	8	6	33	32	32
Arsenal	22	9	4	9	23	22	31
Man City	22	8	6	8	30	24	30
Liverpool	21	8	5	8	35	33	29
Tottenham	22	7	8	7	22	27	29
Middlesbrough	22	6	9	7	33	33	27
Sheff Wed	22	6	9	7	27	29	27
C Palace	22	6	9	7	29	33	27
Leeds	22	6	7	9	33	37	25
Southampton	22	5	9	8	22	26	24
Everton	22	6	5	11	21	30	23
Oldham	20	5	6	9	33	39	21
Sheff Utd	21	5	6	10	18	28	21
Wimbledon	22	4	8	10	26	33	20
Nottm Forest	21	3	6	12	20	33	15

January 9

MANCHESTER UNITED 4

SPURS 1

(Half-time score: 1-0)

United: Schmeichel, Parker, Bruce, Pallister, Irwin, Giggs (Kanchelskis 74), Ince (Phelan 67), McClair, Sharpe, Cantona, Hughes. Sub: Sealey
Scorers: Cantona 40, Irwin 52, McClair 53, Parker 58
Spurs: Thorsvedt, Austin (Bergsson 81), Mabbutt, Ruddock, Edinburgh, Howells, Samways, Nayim (Anderton 70), Allen, Sheringham, Barmby. Sub: Walker
Scorer: Barmby 88
Referee: M Peck (Kendall)
Attendance: 35,648
Weather: Cold

United took time off from their championship exertions to attend to the matter of Bury, 83 places behind Alex Ferguson's multi-million pound side, in the FA Cup. It was to prove a red-letter day for an old stager and a newcomer. In three and a half years Michael Phelan, United's odd job man, had failed to find the target at Old Trafford. Eight minutes into the tie he broke his duck by heading in a cross from teenage debut boy Keith Gillespie.

The dark-haired youngster from Northern Ireland could be well pleased with his contribution but his evening in the limelight was to get even better. Fourteen minutes from time United were looking anxious, the Third division side had made them battle all the way, then up popped Gillespie to ease the strain when his shot squirmed through the hands of Bury goalkeeper Gary Kelly.

"We were in control but we didn't get into top gear. We got what we wanted, a place in the next round, and Bury got a good gate and a game that gave their fans something to shout about," said Fergie.

United's form in the Cup this season had been a low-key affair. In the League, however, it was to be a different story.

Spurs were next in the firing line and, led by the irrepressible Cantona, United looked unstoppable. They grasped the opportunity to go to the top of the pile with both hands in one of their most accomplished and polished performances of the season. For just under an hour they mesmerised a stunned Spurs outfit. Cantona ran the show from the start, creating chances that inspired a superb goalkeeping display from Spurs' Eric Thorstvedt, who denied Brian McClair and Ryan Giggs twice with marvellous stops. The visitors were on the ropes and one down after 40 minutes, with Cantona, who else, the scorer with a floating header at the far post, finishing off a cross from Denis Irwin.

Cantona turned provider in 52 minutes, chipping perfectly as the Spurs defence came out for Irwin to blast United's second. Less than 60 seconds later Thorstvedt again found himself minus a defence as McClair marched through from midfield to hammer the ball home from 25 yards. United were on fire and there was more to follow.

Paul Parker had managed 50 games for United without troubling the scorers, but that was about to change as he banged in goal number four. It was time for United to ease off the throttle. The job had been done with clinical efficiency and the points were safely in the bag. In the dying moments Nick Barmby swooped to head a consolation for Spurs and there was a minor scare when the mercurial Cantona hobbled off the pitch as a precaution against a hamstring tweak.

United were really beginning to warm to the task in hand and Ferguson was keen to play down the significance of the result. He said: "It's nice to go back on top of the League but we've been there before and we're not going to get carried away. We learned that last season and we're not going to start making any predictions now. We face a very tough schedule in March and that's when we will find out just how good this United team is.

"Our players seem to be enjoying their football. We have the confidence of a team on the run. Everybody wants to play. When you play like that the whole place is buzzing. The lads were brilliant today but it's when they face the test that we will really see what we can achieve. We know we have to perform to keep getting results if we are to stay up there. There is a long way to go so don't hold your breath."

League Table After Match

	P	W	D	L	F	A	Pts
MAN UTD	23	11	8	4	34	18	41
Aston Villa	23	11	8	4	34	25	41
Norwich	23	12	5	5	34	34	41
Blackburn	23	10	8	5	34	20	38
Ipswich	23	8	12	3	32	25	36
QPR	22	10	5	7	31	25	35
Chelsea	23	9	8	6	30	26	35
Man City	23	9	6	8	34	26	33
Arsenal	23	9	5	9	24	23	32
Coventry	23	8	8	7	33	33	32
Liverpool	22	8	5	9	36	35	29
Tottenham	23	7	8	8	23	31	29
Leeds	23	7	7	9	35	38	28
Middlesbrough	23	6	9	8	33	34	27
Sheff Wed.	22	6	9	7	27	29	27
C. Palace	23	6	9	8	29	35	27
Everton	23	7	5	11	23	30	26
Oldham	21	6	6	9	35	40	24
Southampton	23	5	9	9	23	28	24
Sheff Utd	22	5	7	10	19	29	22
Wimbledon	23	4	9	10	26	33	21
Nottm Forest	22	4	6	12	21	33	18

Paul Parker celebrates after scoring against Spurs.

January 18

QUEENS PARK RANGERS 1

MANCHESTER UNITED 3
(Half-time score: 1-2)

QPR: Roberts, Bardsley, Peacock (Thompson 70), McDonald, Wilson, Impey, Holloway, Barker, Sinton, Allen, Bailey. Subs: Brevett, Stejskal
Scorer: Allen 42
Booked: McDonald, Barker
United: Schmeichel, Parker, Pallister, Bruce, Irwin, Kanchelskis, Ince, McClair, Sharpe, Hughes (Phelan 9), Giggs. Subs: Lawton, Sealey
Scorers: Ince 26, Giggs 30, Kanchelskis 48
Referee: J Martin (Alton)
Attendance: 21,117
Weather: Wet, windy

Three majestic strikes saw the Reds leap Aston Villa and back to the pinnacle of English football. But this was a controversial clash which made the headlines for all the wrong reasons. United's live Monday evening television appearance gave them two extra days to try and clear their casualty list. However, a tricky encounter with sixth placed Rangers wasn't to be made any easier by the absence of their talisman, Eric Cantona. And it wasn't long before Mark Hughes was to join him on the sidelines.

A fast and furious affair exploded in the 12th minute with an Alan McDonald challenge on the Welshman. Its effect was more like a mugging than a tackle and Hughes departed to have six stitches sewn into a nasty calf wound. Fergie was outraged, McDonald escaped with a yellow card but United regrouped superbly to respond in the best possible way with a magnificent goal.

Wingers were to hold the key in this torrid affair. It was Lee Sharpe who made the first significant impression. He turned inside from the right, his cross partially deflected and Ince produced a spectacular overhead kick which could only have been a blur to the Rangers keeper Tony Roberts. Five minutes later United scored a goal of almost lazy simplicity. Irwin playing the ball through the middle to allow Giggs to run-on and lift the ball expertly beyond the advancing Roberts. Pure skill was triumphing over brawn and brute force but still Rangers' over zealous approach showed little sign of abating. Already furious at Hughes' premature departure, Ferguson blew a gasket when Andy Sinton's crude challenge on Paul Parker passed without so much as a caution let alone a free kick.

Fergie, a man who doesn't mask his emotions, exchanged angry views with his opposite number Gerry Francis and stewards and police stepped in as tempers reached boiling point.

Referee John Martin had spoken with both managers during the half-time interval. Fergie's mood certainly wouldn't have improved following Bradley Allen's goal, scored at the second attempt, two minutes before the break. Three minutes after it, he was all smiles again. Kanchelskis was the scorer, killing off the Rangers with a wonderful finish to a counter-attack prompted by Sharpe and Giggs.

Kanchelskis scores against QPR.

The points were United's. When the going got tough the tough got going. Sadly, the accusations and counter-accusations were to continue into the night. Fergie, clearly ruffled by the events of the evening, blew his top at pressmen. "I've nothing to say about the tackle [Sinton on Parker]. I'm not getting involved. All I'm interested in is the way we performed tonight. The referee was just asking me if I would mind sitting down. I had forgotten what incident it was. You guys go too far, you're a pain in the arse. You don't stop do you."

Rival Francis attempted to play down his head to head with Fergie and tried to inject a spot of humour into a tense night. He said:"It was nothing. Alex Ferguson was after my brand of after-shave and I wasn't interested in giving it to him. Most times I have had no problem with Alex, we've always got on well. I think Sinton and Parker both went for the ball. Maybe I am getting old or my eyesight is going but Alex seems to see things going on out there that I didn't. Maybe he has special glasses.

"I am upset because we are high in the Fairplay League and we are not that type of side. Alex should know better than that. He is entitled to his opinion and I am mine. I spoke to Mark Hughes after the game and he said he got tackled from the back. These things happen in the game week in, week out."

Of course, there are two sides to every argument and manager's often disagree about what happens on the pitch. But the disagreement was irrelevant – Fergie and the three points were safely on their way back to Manchester. Controversy or not, United were bang on target.

League Table After Match

	P	W	D	L	F	A	Pts
MAN UTD	24	12	8	4	37	19	44
Aston Villa	24	12	8	4	39	26	44
Norwich	24	12	6	6	35	36	42
Blackburn	24	11	8	5	35	20	41
Ipswich	24	8	12	4	32	28	36
QPR	23	10	5	8	32	28	35
Arsenal	24	10	5	9	25	23	35
Chelsea	24	9	8	7	30	29	35
Man City	24	9	6	9	34	27	33
Sheff Wed	24	8	9	7	30	29	33
Coventry	24	8	9	7	34	34	33
Liverpool	23	8	5	10	36	37	29
Everton	24	8	5	11	25	30	29
Tottenham	24	7	8	9	23	33	29
Leeds	24	7	7	10	35	40	28
Southampton	24	6	9	9	24	28	27
Middlesbrough	24	6	9	9	34	39	27
C Palace	24	6	9	9	29	36	27
Sheff Utd	23	6	7	10	22	29	25
Wimbledon	24	5	9	10	28	33	24
Oldham	22	6	6	10	35	41	24
Nottm Forest	23	5	6	12	24	33	21

January 27

MANCHESTER UNITED 2

NOTTM FOREST 0

(Half-time score: 0-0)

United: Schmeichel, Parker, Pallister, Bruce, Irwin, Giggs, McClair, Ince, Sharpe, Hughes, Cantona. Subs: Kanchelskis, Phelan, Sealey
Scorers: Ince 47, Hughes 68
Forest: Crossley, Laws, Chettle, Tiler, Williams, Webb, Keane (Crosby 75), Gemmell, Woan (Orlygsson 75), Clough, Bannister. Sub: Marriott
Referee: J Worrall (Warrington)
Attendance: 36,085
Weather: Wet

The FA Cup fourth round clash with Brighton provided a welcome distraction for United. It also gave them time to try and nurse injury victims Hughes, Cantona and Kanchelskis back to full fitness in time for the important clash with Nottingham Forest.

United appeared hungover from the war game at QPR the previous Monday night. Brighton, largely anonymous in their bid to make progress from the second division, were able to stifle United threats with ease before Ryan Giggs' 75th minute blockbuster put the fans out of their misery.

A few days later it was business as usual. Nottingham Forest were proving to be another of the season's surprise teams – for all the wrong reasons. Rock bottom and with Brian Clough, months before his retirement, frantically trying to revive their flagging fortunes, they were not to be underestimated. United, however, performed with the precision and artistry of synchronised swimmers to submerge the tired drowning men of Nottingham. Second half strikes from the fit-again Hughes and the delightful Paul Ince were bare statistics which hid the elaborate embroidery woven around the goals as United's highest gate of the season purred approvingly.

The English game is often condemned as a stage for hard running bodybuilders but here was choreography that would have graced Sadlers Wells. For 45 minutes of this enchanting exchange Forest withstood a quality of football that was close to sublime. And manager's boy Nigel Clough twice had the chance to punish United for their profligacy at the end of the half. It took a cruel deflection for Ince to rectify United's waywardness but then Hughes scored the kind of goal that has become his team's spectacular trademark.

This was United's 10th League game without defeat, eight of them victories, and they had scored 17 goals in the last five of them. The confidence that has been fostered was in sharp contrast to Forest's lack of certainty on the ball. The chains of being bottom weighed heavily. It was a frustration that surfaced 15 minutes from time as tempers rose and Forest's £5m talent, Roy Keane, was substituted after he had clashed with United's Steve Bruce. While the pair were being lectured by Warrington referee Joe Worrall, Paul Ince chose to get involved.

As Keane left the park he was taunted by Ince who was quickly rebuked by Ferguson. "I shouted to Paul to get out of the road. In a situation like that there's always going to be sparks flying, but it was nothing serious." Without the injured Stuart Pearce it was always going to be an evening of overwork and overtime for the Forest defence. To their credit they rolled up their sleeves and made a fist of it.

Gary Pallister, the only United outfield player still to score, almost did twice, Brian Laws clearing one header off the line and Mark Crossley touching the other on to the post. But something or someone had to give and it was Crossley, two minutes after the break, wickedly sent the wrong way when Ince's 35 yarder hit Carl Tiler. Forest could hardly complain, but just to make it absolutely certain no one could question the merit of this win United signed off with a delightful second.

Steve Bruce won the ball inside the Forest half and chipped it forward towards Cantona who, with the deftest of touches, sent in Hughes to volley his 12th goal of the season, in off the underside of the crossbar. "That was a wonderful goal – a killer, typical Sparky Hughes," enthused Fergie. "We had been worried about the chances we were missing in the first half. At the interval we could have been three down after creating maybe eight chances."

Villa were being kept at bay on goal difference but United were buoyed by a haul of 12 points out of 12. However, a setback was just around the corner.

Alex Ferguson in touchline discussion with a police officer.

League Table After Match

	P	W	D	L	F	A	Pts
MAN UTD	25	13	8	4	39	19	47
Aston Villa	25	13	8	4	42	27	47
Norwich	25	13	6	6	39	38	45
Blackburn	25	11	8	6	37	25	41
Coventry	26	10	9	7	42	36	39
Ipswich	25	9	12	4	34	28	39
Man City	25	10	6	9	35	27	36
QPR	24	10	6	8	33	29	36
Chelsea	25	9	9	7	31	30	36
Arsenal	24	10	5	9	25	23	35
Sheff Wed	24	8	9	7	30	29	33
Everton	25	9	5	11	28	31	32
Middlesbrough	25	7	9	9	36	40	30
Liverpool	23	8	5	10	36	37	29
Tottenham	25	7	8	10	23	35	29
Leeds	24	7	7	10	35	40	28
Southampton	25	6	9	10	25	30	27
C Palace	25	6	9	10	31	40	27
Sheff Utd	24	6	7	11	23	32	25
Wimbledon	25	5	9	11	29	36	24
Oldham	24	6	6	12	35	45	24
Nottm Forest	24	5	6	13	24	35	21

January 30

IPSWICH 2

MANCHESTER UNITED 1

(Half-time score: 1-0)

Ipswich: Baker, Bozinoski (Stockwell 87), Whelan, Linighan, Thompson, Johnson, Williams, Dozzell, Yallop, Kiwomya, Guentchev (Wark 87). Sub: Forrest
Scorers: Kiwomya 20, Yallop 48
Booked: Dozzell
United: Schmeichel, Parker, Pallister, Bruce, Irwin, Sharpe (Kanchelskis 67), Ince, McClair, Giggs, Hughes, Cantona. Subs: Phelan, Sealey
Scorer: McClair 84
Booked: Hughes, Pallister
Referee: J Key (Rotherham)
Attendance: 22,068
Weather: Mild

Ipswich Town had earned their place in the inaugural Premier League with considerable style. And they'd moved to sixth place on the back of a solid home record, suffering as few defeats along the way as United. However, they were to go through a roller coaster of emotions during a turbulent campaign. They commanded respect for most of the season, and briefly put in a title challenge during a purple patch. But a slump of the highest magnitude meant relegation fears only vanished after a late April derby success over neighbours Norwich City.

United, unfortunately, arrived at Portman Road with Ipswich in full flight and were to sample the bitter taste of defeat for the first time since Aston Villa in November. Twelve games unbeaten had the effect of spreading fear through the opposition, but on this occasion United were caught out at their own game.

Chris Kiwomya claimed to have got the message from a teammate – and it helped him put a dent in United's title aspirations. "Paul Goddard gave me some advice at half time. He told me they were scared of me and to keep running at them." Kiwomya did, and Fergie's dream team suddenly revealed a flaw as United struggled to keep pace with him.

He scored the first, hit a post and almost won a penalty. The toughest, meanest defence around was suddenly looking vulnerable under the threat of his thrilling breaks. Gary Pallister was lucky to escape after resorting to desperate measures to stop Chris Kiwomya.

John Wark, a veteran of title-winning sides at Anfield, said: "They really were scared of Chris's pace upfront while we stopped their wingers. They are the players who provide the ammunition. Our midfield helped our full backs and it worked. We also won our tackles in midfield and pressed forward which left many of their players out of the game because they are so attack minded. Yet I still fancy them for the title."

Ipswich skipper David Linighan said: "Before the game in the dressing room we looked at their record and joked about whether we really needed to go out there. They are a hell of a side but we have given other people hope by showing they can be beaten."

Everything Ipswich did was designed to prevent Paul Ince, Brian McClair, Mark Hughes and Eric Cantona from showing the sweet touches that have become the trademark of United's title quest.

It was in January last year that United's championship efforts began to wane. But defeat at Ipswich was to be merely proof that they were not yet invincible. "We never thought we were unbeatable," said Hughes who added with foresight, "I can see the title going to the wire, it has concerned us that people were saying it was a foregone conclusion. Today emphasised how difficult it will be and there are a group of teams who can win it."

Midfielder Ince took a positive view: "Last year we were so far out in front and still failed. Being involved in a dog fight will keep us on our toes." It was a scrap Ipswich were to give a miss to in the end. But today, Kiwomya's 15th goal of the season, sliding the ball into an empty net after Schmeichel had failed to clear, had put the skids under United. Two minutes after the interval a rare goal from Frank Yallop, deflected in, made it 2-0.

Only in the last six minutes did United begin to show some form. Brian McClair pulled a goal back and they almost snatched a draw from the jaws of defeat only for Clive Baker to deny Hughes brilliantly in injury time. This time the journey home was to be ponderous ... and a long one.

CLOSE SHAVE ...
Chris Kiwomya hits the post with Peter Schmeichel beaten and Steve bruce grounded.

League Table After Match

	P	W	D	L	F	A	Pts
Norwich	26	14	6	6	40	38	48
MAN UTD	26	13	8	5	40	21	47
Aston Villa	26	13	8	5	42	29	47
Ipswich	26	10	12	4	36	29	42
Blackburn	26	11	8	7	39	28	41
Man City	26	11	6	9	38	29	39
QPR	25	11	6	8	35	30	39
Coventry	27	10	9	8	42	38	39
Sheff Wed.	25	9	9	7	32	29	36
Chelsea	26	9	9	8	31	32	36
Arsenal	24	10	5	9	25	23	35
Everton	26	9	5	12	28	32	32
Tottenham	26	8	8	10	26	36	32
Leeds	25	8	7	10	38	40	31
Southampton	26	7	9	10	27	30	30
Middlesbrough	26	7	9	10	36	43	30
Liverpool	23	8	5	10	36	37	29
Wimbledon	26	6	9	11	31	36	27
C. Palace	26	6	9	11	32	43	27
Sheff Utd	25	6	7	12	24	34	25
Nottm Forest	25	6	6	13	26	35	24
Oldham	25	6	6	13	35	47	24

February 6

MANCHESTER UNITED 2

SHEFFIELD 1

(Half-time score: 0-1)

United: Schmeichel, Parker, Bruce, Pallister, Irwin, Giggs (Kanchelskis 70), McClair, Ince, Sharpe, Cantona, Hughes. Subs: Phelan, Sealey
Scorers: McClair 64, Cantona 80
Sheff Utd: Kelly, Ward, Beesley, Hoyland, Gayle, Cowan, Carr, Kamara (Bradshaw 67), Hartfield, Bryson (Cork 75), Deane. Sub: Kite
Scorer: Carr 7
Booked: Hartfield, Bradshaw
Referee: M Bodenham (East Looe)
Attendance: 36,156
Weather: Wet

Heard the one about the Englishman, the Irishman, the Scotsman and the Welshman? Oh, and the Dane, the Frenchman and the Ukrainian?

Dave 'Harry' Bassett, Sheffield United's chirpy boss, who is usually not short of a quip or three, wasn't laughing after his Blades were cut down at Old Trafford. But he did recognise quality.

As United continued their surge to the championship, the Manchester side could have earned recognition from the League of Nations never mind the Premier League.

But Harry would have been glad to fly the flag for all of them. Well, nearly all of them.

"Eric Cantona's nothing special," said Bassett after the French ace grabbed the winner for United and underlined his reputation as Old Trafford's biggest cult figure for a generation.

"I'm not being derogatory," added Harry. "But Cantona is no more difficult to play against than any of their players. He is no better than the rest of them. I'll put it this way – if I had the chance I'd buy some of the other players in their side before him."

But Harry's backhander did come with a more genuine compliment to a side, inspired by Cantona, who were on their way to ending that 26-year wait for the biggest prize in English soccer.

"The title is wide open, but I wouldn't be surprised if they won it. They haven't been a soft touch for maybe three or four years now. They have a resilience about them. They keep going, though fortune favoured them today. United didn't open us up at all in the first half and even resorted to looking for penalties."

But in that was the implication that United did open up their Sheffield counterparts after half-time. And that's where another member of Old Trafford's Continental Club came in.

Andrei Kanchelskis, former Soviet-born Ukrainian who has opted to play for Russia, got off the bench for the final 20 minutes and handed out a lesson in wing play to young pretender Rayn Giggs, whom he replaced.

Giggs, hugely effective and exciting for most of United's season, produced an afternoon where, for once, the raw teenager in him got the better of the richest talent the English game has seen for years.

For 70 minutes, the young Welshman was so profligate with his final ball that manager Alex Ferguson must have been privately grinding his teeth. But when Fergie's patience with his precocious 19-year-old finally ran out, Kanchelskis was sent on to prove a point and ended up winning three.

Andrei Kanchelskis immediately did what wingers are supposed to do – he drew straight lines in the opposition territory with his direct running and he put the ball where it hurts opponents most.

Kanchelskis swung in a fine cross, full back Mitch Ward's attempted clearance dropped to Cantona and Eric Le Red volleyed the winner.

Earlier, on the hour, it was Cantona's magnificent far post header from Denis Irwin's centre that set up Brian McClair's equaliser to haul a tentative United back into the game.

Old Trafford's anxiety began when Franz Carr skidded past Gary Pallister down the left after eight minutes and somehow angled in Sheffield's goal.

And Brian Deane missed two great chances to further embarrass United, the second right on time as Paul Parker slid a suicidal back pass into his path.

Ferguson later admitted he had never seen such a nervy show early on from his twin pillars at centre back, Pallister and skipper Steve Bruce.

But Cantona's intervention, after a fruitless hour bouncing off Sheffield's five-man defence which no doubt led Bassett to his after-match assessment of the Frenchman, hauled United back as he set up Scotsman McClair. Then came the Ukrainian to aid the Frenchman and sicken the Cockney.

League Table After Match

	P	W	D	L	F	A	Pts
MAN UTD	27	14	8	5	42	22	50
Aston Villa	27	14	8	5	44	29	50
Norwich	26	14	6	6	40	38	48
Coventry	28	11	9	8	44	38	42
Ipswich	27	10	12	5	34	31	42
Blackburn	27	11	8	8	40	30	41
Man City	27	11	7	9	39	30	40
QPR	26	11	7	8	34	31	40
Sheff Wed.	26	10	9	7	36	30	39
Chelsea	27	9	9	9	32	36	36
Arsenal	25	10	5	10	25	24	35
Liverpool	25	9	6	10	37	37	33
Everton	27	9	5	13	29	35	32
Tottenham	26	8	8	10	26	36	32
Leeds	26	8	7	11	38	41	31
Southampton	26	7	9	10	27	30	30
Wimbledon	27	7	9	11	32	34	30
Middlesbrough	27	7	9	11	34	45	30
C. Palace	27	7	9	11	34	44	30
Oldham	26	7	6	13	38	48	27
Nottm Forest	26	6	7	13	26	35	25
Sheff Utd	26	6	7	13	25	34	25

February 8

LEEDS 0

MANCHESTER UNITED 0

(Half-time score: 0-0)

Leeds: Lukic, Sellars (Hodge 85), Dorigo, Batty, Newsome, Whyte, Bowman, Shutt (Strandli 77), Chapman, McAllister, Speed. Sub: Day
United: Schmeichel, Parker, Pallister, Bruce, Irwin, Giggs (Kanchelskis 72), McClair, Ince, Sharpe, Hughes, Cantona. Subs: Phelan, Sealey
Booked: Pallister, Cantona
Referee: K Morton (Bury St Edmunds)
Attendance: 34,166
Weather: Cold

There will always be a place for Leeds in Eric Cantona's heart.

Cantona returned to Elland Road for the first time since his £1.2 million move and found that hell hath no fury like a football club scorned.

The Leeds fans subjected him to derision that could not have been worse had their local served up cold Yorkshire pudding and a flat pint of Tetley's for Sunday lunch.

It was hard not to divorce the Cantona cameo from a match played with all the old intensity of trans-Pennine pugilists. And for United there was also the small score to be settled of *that* championship, which the Yorkshire side stole from United the season before.

Yet Cantona took compassion on the club that made him a hero and for whom he as good as won the title, like he would for United. Twice he could have secured the points that would have given United a three-point lead at the top of the Premier League.

But twice he failed, and to the ecstasy of most in the 34,166 crowd, he also collected a yellow card.

There has been plenty of traffic between the two clubs in years past – Strachan and Giles to Leeds, McQueen and Jordan to United – which has caused barely a ripple. But Leeds fans saw Cantona's move quite simply as an act of betrayal – a move brought into sharper focus by the loss of form of the reigning champions and the resurgence of a Cantona-inspired United.

But while Cantona fleetingly involved himself with a ferocious struggle between the sides, he still made the headlines – and an FA court, charged with bringing the game into disrepute.

That apart, though, this was not Cantona's kind of match. It was more Hulk Hogan meets the Ultimate Warrior. And no one won.

Leeds strung five talented men across midfield and attacked from deep, a tactic which unsettled the Manchester defence.

Gary McAllister, Gary Speed and David Batty launched a long-range offensive on Peter Schmeichel's goal, raining in shots from anything up to 30 yards.

They bared their teeth to win possession and fought Paul Ince and Brian McClair in a bone-crunching battle.

But if Leeds had the edge in possession, United created the

Let the party begin. A thunderbolt from Giggs prompted the first of many celebrations on the night United were crowned 'champions'.

*The championship was already won but for the sake of
the faithful who had crossed continents to be there,
they had to win again: vs. Blackburn, May 3.*

*Worthy Champions. After 26 years it feels pretty good
for captains and manager alike.*

Brian McClair, Steve Bruce,
Gary Pallister, Bryan Robson,
Denis Irwin, Andrei Kanchelskis,
Ryan Giggs, Paul Ince.
May 3 1993.

The trophy looked different in those days and so did George and Bobby, but there wasn't a dry eye in the house 26 years on.

For Bryan Robson this was probably his last chance of a championship medal. Almost certainly with a large dose of divine intervention it was he who scored the final, and 67th, goal of the campaign and the celebrations began all over again.

better chances through their young wing wonders, Lee Sharpe and Ryan Giggs.

Ironically, it was another youngster, Robert Bowman, who withstood that assault. Making his debut at right back, the 17-year-old was a product of Manchester United's own School of Excellence and in this game proved that United might have continued his education.

However, as United turned up the heat, Cantona should have given them the lead in the 18th minute. Sharpe's glorious crossfield pass found the Frenchman and, with keeper John Lukic off his line, he tried the cheekiest of chips which dropped a foot over the bar.

In the 27th minute, Lukic produced a stunning acrobatic save, tipping over Chris Whyte's deflection off McClair's shot.

Lee Chapman had Leeds' best chance from Batty's mis-hit strike, but he shot tamely at Schmeichel. The Danish keeper went on to make good saves from Tony Dorigo's 30-yard free-kick and, in the last minute, from a McAllister header by the foot of his post.

It was a breathless finish to a breathless match full of Oohs and Aahs … but not all of them for Cantona.

RETURN OF THE EXILE …
Cantona in the thick of things
back at Elland Road.

League Table After Match

	P	W	D	L	F	A	Pts
MAN UTD	28	14	9	5	42	22	51
Aston Villa	27	14	8	5	44	29	50
Norwich	26	14	6	6	40	38	48
Coventry	28	11	9	8	44	38	42
Ipswich	27	10	12	5	36	31	42
Blackburn	27	11	8	8	40	30	41
Man City	27	11	7	9	39	30	40
QPR	26	11	7	8	36	31	40
Sheff Wed	26	10	9	7	35	30	39
Chelsea	27	9	9	9	32	35	36
Arsenal	25	10	5	10	25	24	35
Tottenham	27	9	8	10	30	38	35
Liverpool	25	9	6	10	37	37	33
Leeds	27	8	8	11	38	41	32
Everton	27	9	5	13	29	35	32
Wimbledon	27	7	9	11	32	36	30
Southampton	27	7	9	11	29	34	30
Middlesbrough	27	7	9	11	36	45	30
C. Palace	27	7	9	11	34	44	30
Oldham	26	7	6	13	38	48	27
Nottm Forest	26	6	7	13	26	35	25
Sheff Utd	26	6	7	13	25	36	25

February 20

MANCHESTER UNITED 2

SOUTHAMPTON 1

(Half-time score: 0-0)

United: Schmeichel, Parker, Bruce, Pallister, Irwin, Sharpe, Ince, McClair, Giggs, Hughes, Cantona. Subs: Phelan, Kanchelskis, Sealey
Scorer: Giggs 81, 82
Booked: Hughes, Cantona
Soton: Flowers, Kenna, Hall, Monkou, Benali, Dodd, Widdrington, Maddison, Adams, Dowie, Le Tissier (Banger 65). Subs: Moore, Andrews
Scorer: Banger 77
Booked: Widdrington, Hall
Referee: R Lewis (Gt Bookham)
Attendance: 36,257
Weather: Cold, drizzle

Champions, whether they be a Mansell, a Muhammad Ali or a Manchester United, do not perform at their peak all the time. But they do have the Edge.

What sets them apart is that little extra, which crucially, will always surface when times look rocky.

United's collective will to win proved their Edge over their rivals in the end. But as United suffered a title twitch during the late winter of 1993, the Edge then was found in the razor-sharp form of Ryan Giggs.

Six days before this match, United had crashed out of the FA Cup just when the bookies were beginning to lay odds on the Double.

With five minutes remaining of their fifth round tie at Sheffield United, Steve Bruce missed a penalty that would have earned them a replay. Yet, although United were missing Cantona – away on World Cup duty – any reward from Bramall Lane might have merely disguised a form wobble that was growing marked by the week.

The 2-1 defeat in Sheffield, followed by 82 minutes of abysmal effort at home to Southampton, underlined the fact that United were beginning to display a worrying dip below their own high standards.

And then they produced their Edge.

Southampton keeper Tim Flowers later dubbed Ryan Giggs the Sidewinder and spoke for members of his profession past and present when he said: "Speaking as a football fan, I thought he was brilliant. Speaking as a member of the goalkeepers' union, he's a nightmare."

It is appropriate that Old Trafford, where every square yard has been trodden by great attackers, should now be graced by the flying feet of Giggs.

Flowers added: "I was unfortunate in not being old enough to see George Best. But when they compare the two Giggs must be somewhere near him because he was pure magic today."

And as Giggs reduced Southampton's resistance to rubble twice in the space of a minute, the youngster, blessed with Best's ability to attack defenders right, left and centre, proved he was learning to match the great man's flair for finishing too.

Flowers could hardly believe it as two sublime examples of the Giggs technique plundered the points in the last eight minutes of a match that was going nowhere for United. Much of the game – there were 11 minutes of stoppages – resembled a traffic light stuck on red.

But Southampton, cussed and uncomfortable opponents, looked to have broken through the jam on 78 minutes. Substitute Nicky Banger, outstripping Gary Pallister, rammed in an angled shot that crept inside Peter Schmeichel's near post.

But then Giggs struck and Flowers was in the firing line. "He was one on one for the first and had too much time to finish," said the goalkeeper. "He was throwing stacks of dummies at me and in the end just curled his foot around the ball and whipped it into the corner."

Giggs' second goal, less than 60 seconds later, saw the winger run across Flowers and throw him off balance before shooting the other way.

"Whether he knew I couldn't push off the ground to make the save I don't know. But I wouldn't put it past Giggs to have done it deliberately.

"Ryan goes down the pitch like a snake, sidewinding all the way. You just don't know if he'll come inside and shoot or dip outside and cross the ball."

Alex Ferguson, continuing his protectionist policy over his young star, would only say: "He's maturing bit by bit and we'll see what the finished article is in four years."

Flowers and his goalkeeping chums can hardly wait.

Giggs cracks home a power drive past Southampton keeper Tim Flowers.

League Table After Match

	P	W	D	L	F	A	Pts
Aston Villa	30	16	8	6	47	31	56
MAN UTD	29	15	9	5	44	23	54
Norwich	28	15	6	7	42	42	51
QPR	28	12	8	8	39	32	44
Ipswich	29	10	14	5	37	32	44
Sheff Wed	27	11	9	7	37	31	42
Coventry	29	11	9	9	44	40	42
Blackburn	28	11	8	9	40	30	41
Tottenham	29	11	8	10	36	39	41
Man City	28	11	7	10	40	32	40
Arsenal	27	11	5	11	26	25	38
Chelsea	29	9	10	10	32	36	37
Wimbledon	29	9	9	11	35	36	36
Southampton	30	9	9	12	35	37	36
Liverpool	28	9	8	11	38	39	35
Leeds	29	9	8	12	40	45	35
C. Palace	29	8	9	12	36	46	33
Everton	29	9	5	15	31	39	32
Middlesbrough	29	7	9	13	37	49	30
Nottm Forest	27	7	7	13	28	36	28
Sheff Utd	28	7	7	14	27	38	28
Oldham	28	7	6	15	38	51	27

February 27

MANCHESTER UNITED 3

MIDDLESBROUGH 0

(Half-time score: 1-0)

United: Schmeichel, Parker, Bruce, Pallister, Irwin, Giggs, McClair, Ince, Sharpe, Hughes, Cantona. Subs: Kanchelskis, Sealey, Phelan
Scorers: Giggs 21, Irwin 78, Cantona 85
Middlesbrough: Pears, Morris, Mustoe, Whyte, Phillips, Hendrie, Peake, Kamara, Mustoe (Slaven 72), Wright, Wilkinson. Subs: Ironside, Kernaghan
Referee: K Hackett (Sheffield)
Attendance: 36,251
Weather: Snow, sleet, cold

The fans went through agonising moments at times, with United fighting to hang on to their form as the title run-in approached in earnest.

Against Middlesbrough, there was a nervousness that rippled around the stadium like a Mexican Wave with DTs.

And the English game's biggest audience clearly showed that championship neurosis was getting to them in their treatment of Lee Sharpe.

It was Sharpe's bad luck that when he was put clean through after the half-time break, it was on a day when his confidence was lacking.

The fans' response to his bungled effort was predictable ... even though the 1992-93 season would, ultimately, prove to be a renaissance for the 21-year-old who was on his way back after long bouts of illness and injury.

Sharpe may have suffered in comparison with the brilliant Ryan Giggs, whose 22nd-minute lightning bolt put United one up. But it should not be forgotten that it was only two or three years previously that Sharpe had been the teenage prodigy and earning the 'New Best' headlines that were coming Giggs' way now.

Middlesbrough's busy on-loan midfielder Chris Kamara was in a unique position that day to judge the mood at Old Trafford, having played for Sheffield United there at the start of February.

Kamara could not help noticing that with the first championship in 26 years beckoning, the place was definitely twitching.

Not until Denis Irwin and Eric Cantona finally cut through the opposition blockade in the last ten minutes did relief flood the stands and the stadium come alive.

As a Leeds player the year before, Kamara basked in the blast of fanaticism that rolled from the terraces at Elland Road as Leeds leapfrogged to the title.

Said Kamara: "Eric Cantona told me on the pitch before the game how disappointed he was with the crowd's reaction to his return there. But at Leeds the fans are worth a goal start. They're so fanatical about their team, they just don't see the opposition doing a thing.

"There is so much expectation around Old Trafford, however, it seems to get to the crowd. They need something special to get them going."

That happened in the last 11 minutes. Left back Denis Irwin, one of the best dead-ball specialists in the game, showed the depth of skill at Old Trafford with a pair of marvellous free-kicks.

One struck a post, the other made it 2-0 and effectively sealed United's points in the 79th minute.

And only the bravery of Stephen Pears in Boro's goal stopped Cantona adding two more goals to the fine effort he smashed in off the goalkeeper's legs five minutes from time.

But the fans should have known there was more to come following Giggs' opener. With little backlift and practically in line with the posts, he stunned Boro with a first-half shot that flashed across Pears.

"He has made himself the key man," added Kamara. "Giggs was their best player in the FA Cup tie at Sheffield United and some of the stuff he did today was unbelievable."

Dennis Irwin (left) with another of his thunderbolts for United's second goal.

League Table After Match

	P	W	D	L	F	A	Pts
Aston Villa	31	17	8	6	48	31	59
MAN UTD	30	16	9	5	47	23	57
Norwich	28	15	6	7	42	42	51
Sheff Wed.	29	12	10	7	40	33	46
Blackburn	28	12	8	8	42	30	44
QPR	30	12	8	10	41	36	44
Ipswich	30	10	14	6	37	33	44
Tottenham	30	12	8	10	39	41	44
Man City	30	12	7	11	43	34	43
Coventry	30	11	10	9	44	40	43
Arsenal	28	11	6	11	26	25	39
Southampton	31	10	9	12	38	39	39
Leeds	31	10	9	12	41	45	39
Chelsea	30	9	10	11	32	38	37
Liverpool	29	9	9	11	39	40	36
Wimbledon	30	9	9	12	35	37	36
C. Palace	30	8	10	12	36	46	34
Everton	30	9	6	15	33	41	33
Nottm Forest	29	8	7	14	29	38	31
Sheff Utd	30	8	7	15	31	41	31
Middlesbrough	30	7	9	14	37	52	30
Oldham	30	7	7	16	40	55	28

March 6

LIVERPOOL 1

MANCHESTER UNITED 2

(Half-time score: 0-1)

Liverpool: James, Jones, Wright, Nicol, Bjornebye, Walters (Burrows 79), Redknapp, Stewart (Rush 44), Barnes, McManaman, Hutchison. Sub: Hooper
Scorer: Rush 50
United: Schmeichel, Parker, Bruce, Pallister, Irwin, Kanchelskis, Ince, McClair, Sharpe, Hughes, Giggs. Subs: Phelan, Dublin, Sealey
Scorers: Hughes 42, McClair 56
Referee: R Milford (Bristol)
Attendance: 44,374
Weather: Cold, overcast

There's little Manchester United fans enjoy more than to beat Liverpool on their own patch, or anywhere else for that matter. United have had their fair share of success at fortress Anfield over the years though they hadn't scored in five visits. But things ain't what they used to be.

This was a contest offering compelling evidence that the power and the glory that was once Liverpool's is now flooding to the other end of the East Lancashire Road. Even the Kop faithful in a 44,000 plus crowd, England's biggest club attendance this season, sensed the days of empire were over and that a Premier League survival battle lay ahead.

They were outwitted by United's travelling hordes, whose wicked delight at Liverpool's fall from grace prompted them to chant 'Souness must stay' as their gallant heroes resumed control at the top with goals from Mark Hughes and Brian McClair. It was an irony that Liverpool were unhinged by their former Manchester City player Paul Stewart, a boyhood United supporter. Stewart, under pressure from the bubbling Lee Sharpe, attempted a clearance only for the ball to fall kindly for Denis Irwin. He allowed Ryan Giggs to supply the cross and Mark Hughes rose to head home and end United's barren run at Anfield.

McClair scores with a header, leaving the Liverpool defence stranded.

Grateful United had repelled Liverpool's spirited assault in the opening half hour thanks to some good fortune. Paul Parker spectacularly volleyed a Mark Walters cross on to his own crossbar in one frantic incident and Peter Schmeichel enhanced his growing reputation with a stupendous save. That moment of goalkeeping magic, which saw him somehow keep out Don Hutchison's venomous shot, was hailed by both managers. They also saluted Ian Rush's 291st Liverpool goal.

Rush had previously been dropped by boss Graeme Souness and feared for his future with the club. He confessed: "I think I was playing well before and I have always given 100 per cent but I got dropped. I was told that in the previous three matches I never had a shot at goal yet I've always been told to play the easy ball, to pass to the man in the best position. I've been brought up at Liverpool to think of it as a team game. But now, for the first time in all my years here I feel I have to play for myself to get a place in the side.

"However, Liverpool are more important that anything. More important than me or the manager. I woke up on Saturday morning not expecting to be in the 14. Then I read in the papers that I was going to be substitute but it wasn't confirmed to me until 2 p.m.." The Welshman had once gone 23 games without scoring against the reds, but in the 50th minute he made it three in successive matches, conjuring up a dazzling effort which briefly threatened to check United's march.

Even the giant Schmeichel was left helpless as the new single-minded Rush lashed in the equaliser. Rush had a point to prove to Souness and the satisfaction was all his. Thankfully for United he didn't push it, though it was a close call. Brian McClair had swooped from close in to restore United's lead but in the dying minutes they were pegged back. Inevitably, Rush was in the thick of it and mighty Schmeichel was forced into a desperate double take to prevent him from sneaking a point.

Souness, with only one win from 14 games, said: "United must have a great chance of wining the title, but we've got something far more important to worry about." March was to be a crucial month for United and they couldn't have asked for a better start. However, in the weeks ahead Fergie was to do his own share of worrying.

League Table After Match

	P	W	D	L	F	A	Pts
MAN UTD	31	17	9	5	49	24	60
Aston Villa	31	17	8	6	48	31	59
Norwich	31	15	8	8	44	46	53
QPR	31	13	8	10	44	37	47
Sheff Wed	30	12	10	8	40	34	46
Coventry	31	12	10	9	45	40	46
Blackburn	30	12	9	9	43	32	45
Ipswich	31	10	14	7	37	34	44
Tottenham	31	12	8	11	39	47	44
Man City	30	12	7	11	43	34	43
Southampton	32	11	9	12	40	40	42
Arsenal	30	11	7	12	27	27	40
Chelsea	31	10	10	11	33	38	40
Leeds	31	10	9	12	41	45	39
Liverpool	30	9	9	12	40	42	36
Wimbledon	31	9	9	13	34	38	36
Everton	31	10	6	15	36	42	36
C. Palace	31	8	11	12	37	47	35
Sheff Utd	31	9	7	15	37	41	34
Middlesbrough	31	8	9	14	38	52	33
Nottm Forest	30	8	8	14	30	38	32
Oldham	30	7	7	16	40	56	28

March 9

OLDHAM 1

MANCHESTER UNITED 0

(Half-time score: 1-0)

Oldham: Gerrard, Fleming, Halle, Jobson, Pointon (Redmond 75), Bernard, Milligan, Henry, Brennan, Adams, Olney. Subs: Palmer, Keeley
Scorer: Adams 26
Booked: Henry, Halle
United: Schmeichel, Parker, Bruce, Pallister, Irwin, Kanchelskis (Dublin 73), Ince, McClair, Sharpe, Hughes, Giggs. Subs: Phelan, Sealey
Booked: Hughes
Referee: G Ashby (Worcester)
Attendance: 17,106
Weather: Dry, cold

Manchester United's roller-coaster season sped on to Boundary Park on a gloomy Tuesday night and promptly came off the rails. Having beaten Liverpool at Anfield three days before, they just couldn't impose their superior skills on a relegation-threatened Oldham side 32 points beneath them in the Premier League and prepared to battle for their footballing lives. It was Oldham's first win against United in 18 years.

But if it was a disappointing night for United fans no-one could deny Oldham's affable manager Joe Royle his finest hour in a desperate season. Royle, in fact, phoned United's rivals Villa immediately after the game to demand a case of champagne.

Villa manager Ron Atkinson had phoned Royle earlier in the day and had "dared" his Oldham side to beat their rich neighbours from just 10 miles down the road and do Villa a favour in the title race. It was a typical piece of flamboyant Atkinson psychology. And it worked!

Royle explained after the game: "Big Ron said we hadn't the bottle to beat United. I said he could send me a bottle of champagne if we did – he replied he'd make it a whole case."

The sparkling stuff would still have been safe in Atkinson's cellar at his luxury Worcestershire home if United had not forgotten how to hurt opponents in the areas that matter. A Neil Adams header rewarded a hard night's work for Oldham. Though Brian McClair hit the bar 20 minutes from time, Alex Ferguson's stars couldn't make an effective dent.

Ferguson's reaction? "It was the survival of the fittest," he said. "Once we lost that goal, Oldham fought for their lives. We've no complaints – we had enough of the ball in the box, but didn't show much composure. It was still a terrible goal to concede – an un-Manchester United affair. We shouldn't give away a goal like that at the back post."

Winger Adams, who had scored twice in the dying minutes to pull Oldham back to 2-2 at Everton in their previous game, planted a firm downward header inside the post from Mark Brennan's 26th minute corner.

Oldham's Neil Adams (No 7) scores the winner at Boundary Park.

Oldham centre-back Richard Jobson's challenge unhinged Peter Schmeichel so much that the League's best keeper hardly moved for the ball.

In the 73rd minute Ferguson introduced big Dion Dublin into the action for the first time since the £1 million striker broke an ankle at Old Trafford in September. Dublin replaced Andrei Kanchelskis, who left with the look of a man who knew he would be back on the bench when banned Eric Cantona returned for the title showdown with Aston Villa at Old Trafford the following Sunday. United even threw centre-back Steve Bruce into attack late on, but the Old Trafford skipper confessed: "We shot ourselves in the foot."

League Table After Match

	P	W	D	L	F	A	Pts
MAN UTD	32	17	9	6	49	25	60
Aston Villa	31	17	8	6	48	31	59
Norwich	31	15	8	8	44	46	53
QPR	31	13	8	10	44	37	47
Blackburn	31	12	10	9	43	32	46
Sheff Wed	30	12	10	8	40	34	46
Coventry	32	12	10	10	45	41	46
Ipswich	31	10	14	7	37	34	44
Tottenham	31	12	8	11	39	47	44
Man City	30	12	7	11	43	34	43
Southampton	33	11	10	12	40	40	43
Arsenal	30	11	7	12	27	27	40
Chelsea	31	10	10	11	33	38	40
Wimbledon	32	10	9	13	34	30	39
Leeds	31	10	9	12	41	45	39
Everton	32	11	6	15	34	42	39
Liverpool	30	9	9	12	40	42	36
C. Palace	31	8	11	12	37	47	35
Sheff Utd	31	9	7	15	37	41	34
Middlesbrough	32	8	9	15	34	54	33
Nottm Forest	30	8	8	14	30	38	32
Oldham	31	8	7	16	41	56	31

March 14

MANCHESTER UNITED 1

ASTON VILLA 1

(Half-time score: 0-0)

United: Schmeichel, Parker, Bruce, Pallister, Irwin, Giggs, Ince, McClair, Sharpe, Cantona, Hughes. Subs: Robson, Kanchelskis, Sealey
Scorer: Hughes 57
Villa: Bosnich, Barrett, McGrath, Teale, Small, Houghton, Parker (Daley 66), Richardson, Staunton, Saunders, Yorke. Subs: Cox, Spink
Scorer: Staunton 53
BOOKED: Teale
Referee: A Gunn (South Chailey)
Attendance: 36,163
Weather: Sunny

An Old Trafford old boy turned up to deny United in what, with just nine games left, was billed as the title showdown. Mark Bosnich was at Old Trafford for three years, where he played three League games, one in 1989-90 and two in '90-91. Then he returned home disillusioned because he could not get a work permit. He spent his life eating well, enjoying the beach life and training three times a week while playing for Sydney Croatia. He was going nowhere.

And then United's former coach, Bryan Whitehouse, noting that Bosnich had married a Manchester girl, rescued his career by bringing him back to Villa. And Bosnich repaid the compliment in this absorbing confrontation, rescuing Villa with a series of magnificent saves from Eric Cantona, Dennis Irwin and Ryan Giggs. It was Bosnich's hour of glory and one which at one time he never dreamed he would experience. He explained: "Back in Sydney I got very low, working as a labourer for my father who makes glass-fibre swimming pools. Australia is a very hard place in which to discipline yourself. You can go overboard if you don't check yourself. Never did I think I'd be back at Old Trafford one day playing in a game like this."

United old boy Paul McGrath gets in a crunching tackle on Hughes.

United, however, their imaginative, penetrative play at its sharpest, could have had four penalties, though it's never easy winning penalties in big games as Ferguson graphically noted: "You need to shoot someone with a Tommy gun to get a penalty in a big game." Ferguson later saluted his men, saying: "In the modern trend of football my United are a breath of fresh air. Cantona has such vision. I'd pay to see him play." But it would have been tough on Villa if they'd lost, for no team which produces the kind of goal Steve Staunton fashioned so violently in the 54th minute deserves to lose the day. It was one of the goals of the season.

Kevin Richardson, playing with steel and passion, won another blockbuster tackle at the edge of the box and Brian Small picked up the loose ball. He fed it wide to Staunton surging forward on the left wing. From two yards beyond the right corner of United's 18-yard box Staunton's shot went like a bullet just inside the crossbar and far post. Such a penetrating strike would have destroyed many lesser sides but to United it was just a signal to step up the aggression.

It took just five minutes to level the score and United once more were controlling the game. Irwin, probably the most improved full-back in the Premier League, set up the goal. Brian McClair back-heeled into the Irishman's path and Irwin's beautifully struck cross was headed back by Eric Cantona for Mark Hughes to steer it crisply past Bosnich.

Villa also survived two penalty appeals, one when Brian Small challenged McClair, the other when Earl Barrett appeared to wrestle Lee Sharpe to the ground. Shaun Teale was also booked by referee Alf Gunn for another wrestling match with Cantona. But if Villa were constantly rocked on their heels they never lost their footing, never lost their shape and never lost their danger. Dwight Yorke and Dean Saunders always threatened to slip behind United's defence. Richardson was outstanding in midfield but Gary Parker had an off-day and was replaced in the 67th minute by Tony Daley. Daley's searing pace, however, failed to unsettle Pallister and Bruce, by far the most solid defensive pairing in the League.

Yet no-one played harder than Paul McGrath, the all-purpose defender-cum-midfielder who was rejected by United but won the players' Player of the Year award in 1993 by a country mile. In the end United lacked the clinical finishing needed to pierce their closest rivals. But the awesome quality of the game convinced English soccer fans of one thing – the Premier League's first title was bound for either Manchester or Birmingham.

BEST OF PALS …
Giggs, Ince and Cantona mob
goal-scorer Mark Hughes.

League Table After Match

	P	W	D	L	F	A	Pts
MAN UTD	33	17	10	6	50	26	61
Aston Villa	33	17	10	6	49	32	61
Norwich	33	17	8	8	46	46	59
Sheff Wed	31	13	10	8	41	34	49
QPR	33	13	8	12	45	40	47
Blackburn	31	12	10	9	43	32	46
Man City	32	13	7	12	44	35	46
Coventry	34	12	10	12	45	44	46
Southampton	34	12	10	12	44	43	46
Tottenham	32	12	9	11	39	47	45
Ipswich	33	10	14	9	40	39	44
Arsenal	31	12	7	12	29	27	43
Chelsea	32	11	10	11	35	39	43
Liverpool	32	11	9	12	43	43	42
Wimbledon	33	11	9	13	40	40	42
Leeds	32	11	9	12	42	45	42
Everton	34	12	6	16	40	44	42
C. Palace	31	8	11	12	37	47	35
Sheff Utd	32	9	7	16	37	42	34
Middlesbrough	33	8	9	16	39	56	33
Nottm Forest	31	8	8	15	30	42	32
Oldham	32	8	7	17	41	56	31

March 20

MAN CITY 1

MANCHESTER UNITED 1

(Half-time score: 0-0)

City: Coton, Hill, Vonk, Curle, Phelan, Flitcroft, Reid, Holden, White, Quinn, Sheron. Subs: Quigley, Ingebrigtsen, Margetson
Scorer: Quinn 57
Booked: Reid, Curle
United: Schmeichel, Parker, Bruce, Pallister, Irwin, Giggs, Ince, McClair, Sharpe, Cantona, Hughes.Subs: Robson, Sealey, Kanchelskis
Scorer: Cantona 68
Booked: Hughes
Referee: R Hunt (Darlington)
Attendance: 37,136
Weather: Fair

OOH LA LA …
Lee Sharpe in raptures after
Cantona's equaliser.

Defeat at Oldham, a point rescued at home to Aston Villa and now a Manchester Derby which threatened to be the most significant since Denis Law's back heel relegated United to the second division. More than 37,000 packed Maine Road for a lunchtime squabble that dramatically swung one way and then the other. United came from behind and squandered chances to win it. Two points went down the drain and Villa were again clear at the helm.

The script had gone awry once more, United's fluency had evaporated, they desperately need reviving. Now Alex Ferguson was to face the trickiest decision of his career. Should he bring back Bryan Robson for the vital last eight games of the title trail? United's one-man motivator looked a bit like a man in a ball and chain as he shuffled up and down the touch-line from the bench. Robbo didn't get a whiff of the action and at 36 will only get a look in as a defensive midfielder should Fergie decide to allow him off the leash.

Fergie had three days to decide whether Robbo was still the man to galvanise United. Arsenal were next, and United realised they should have been points nearer the ultimate goal. City's Tony Coton knew why pulses were quickening and stomachs tightening in the Old Trafford dressing room. Coton said: "United will be thinking the sort of chances they had here should have been tucked away if they are going to win the league. I'm not saying they won't do it. But if they don't they could well look back in May and say the chances they wasted today cost them dear."

Outwardly, Ferguson remained calm, even chirpy about the prospect of another late season trip to the precipice. But he knew Eric Cantona and Ryan Giggs wasted their advantage in an absorbing tussle. The Frenchman stretched Coton into a stunning stop with a downward header. Yet Cantona was then casual to the point of exasperation with another chance inside the six-yard box which he stroked straight at the keeper.

And with one of the best left feet in the league at his command, Giggs proceeded to use it to spray shots everywhere but on target. Coton summed it up: "He let me off the hook. He should have at least forced me to make a save. You have got to hurt the opposition in those situations and Giggs will be disappointed he didn't." It was

HEADMASTER …
Cantona powers home a rocket
to equalise at Maine Road.

predictable that City, driven by Peter Reid's brain and 21-year-old Garry Flitcroft's lung power, should make United pay for such laxity. When winger Rick Holden got in a cross after an hour, Niall Quinn punished United with a well directed header.

That was showman Cantona's cue to respond, rising with majestic power and purpose to head in Lee Sharpe's cross nine minutes later. City's back four cried foul, Cantona was offside they claimed. But the scales were balanced as Keith Curle barged over Mark Hughes in the box – no penalty! "I didn't think it was a penalty at the time. But our coach Sam Ellis said to us afterwards that if we felt their goal was offside perhaps we were lucky the ref didn't give them a spot kick," admitted Coton. Hughes, though, did not think for one moment United's title surge would be brushed aside so unfairly. He said… "There are no alarm bells ringing. The main difference this time is that we are creating chances – last season we weren't."

United skipper Steve Bruce had no doubt. He said: "Last season's experience will drive us on. We have learned from that. We're not in a position at the moment where real questions are being asked. The moment of truth has yet to come."

Perhaps so, but if there weren't fireworks against Arsenal, would Fergie call on Captain Marvel?

League Table After Match

	P	W	D	L	F	A	Pts
Aston Villa	34	18	10	6	51	32	64
MAN UTD	34	17	11	6	51	27	62
Norwich	35	18	8	9	49	49	62
Sheff Wed	32	13	10	9	41	36	49
QPR	34	13	9	12	47	42	48
Blackburn	32	12	11	9	44	33	47
Man City	33	13	8	12	45	36	47
Coventry	35	12	11	12	45	44	47
Arsenal	32	13	7	12	33	30	46
Southampton	35	12	10	13	47	47	46
Tottenham	33	12	10	11	40	48	46
Wimbledon	34	12	9	13	43	40	45
Liverpool	33	12	9	12	44	43	45
Ipswich	34	10	15	9	40	39	45
Chelsea	34	11	12	11	37	41	45
Leeds	32	11	9	12	42	45	42
Everton	35	12	6	17	40	45	42
C Palace	33	9	12	12	39	48	39
Sheff Utd	33	9	7	17	37	43	34
Middlesbrough	34	8	10	16	40	57	34
Nottm Forest	32	8	8	16	30	45	33
Oldham	33	8	8	17	43	58	32

March 24

MANCHESTER UNITED 0
_____

ARSENAL 0

(Half-time score: 0-0)

United: Schmeichel, Parker, Bruce, Pallister, Irwin, Giggs, McClair, Ince, Sharpe, Cantona, Hughes (Robson 77).Subs: Kanchelskis, Sealey

Arsenal: Seaman, Dixon, Linighan, Adams (Hillier 89), Keown, Carter (Parlour 60), Morrow, Jensen, Merson, Campbell, Wright. Sub: Miller

Referee: V Callow (Solihull)

Attendance: 37,301

Weather: Cold, dry

Little changed. Robson continued to bide his time on the substitute's bench and United remained in the grip of neurosis that led to them blowing the title a year ago. George Graham's Gunners might so easily have opened deeper wounds in Old Trafford's championship ambitions as the ground was flooded with relief as much as exasperation.

United had an eleven day break before confronting the erratic Norwich City in what was to prove the turning point of the season, and Fergie had much hard work to get through. United's last four games had produced just three points and two goals – a statistic which was beginning to signal a buckling title campaign.

On a night when conviction was needed, United had to thank the shovel hands of Peter Schmeichel for the single point. The big Danish keeper had no right to retrieve the ball as Arsenal's speedy

Kevin Campbell moved on to Paul Merson's pass after just six minutes with Old Trafford's 37,301 crowd holding its breath.

But Schmeichel demonstrated his magnificent anticipation, scooping the ball out of Campbell's midriff with his left hand and United were relieved again. Schmeichel, panned by his defence for the goal that United conceded in the Maine Road draw with Manchester City, also spreadeagled himself to foil England striker Ian Wright just before the half-time break.

Eric Cantona, wriggling his way into the Arsenal penalty area, was always United's best hope of the goal they so desperately needed to regain their momentum in the chase for glory. His best effort, prior to the break, was dealt with by David Seaman. The reality was that the best chances were on the toe ends of the Gunners.

Even when United, wound up by a crowd who had suddenly heard that Aston Villa, leaders before the kick-off, were trailing at Norwich, took the game to Arsenal in the final 45 minutes they did little to suggest they were capable of snatching all three points.

Alex Ferguson had chided his club's fans for their growing apprehension. In the match programme he wrote: "At times they strike me as apprehensive. My advice is that they should sit back, relax and enjoy it. I most certainly take exception to one or two hints around at the moment that our biggest problem is keeping cool. It seems as if it has become fashionable to suggest that United might suddenly become nervous and that is rubbish."

Yet goal poacher Campbell, seeing a shot screw off Gary Pallister's foot, and Merson, firing a superb dipping 30 yard effort against the crossbar, would have tweaked the nerve ends of even the most confident home fans. With 14 minutes left Ferguson played his wild card, at last introducing Bryan Robson into the fray for Hughes.

Old Trafford's Captain Marvel did his best but there was never going to be more than a point in it. It had been a poor month for United, dropping nine points out of a possible 15 … anything but title form. April was to be little easier, but it was time for United to do or die.

*Hughes tries to force a way
through against Arsenal.*

League Table After Match

	P	W	D	L	F	A	Pts
Aston Villa	31	17	8	6	48	31	59
MAN UTD	30	16	9	5	47	23	57
Norwich	28	15	6	7	42	42	51
Sheff Wed	29	12	10	7	40	33	46
Blackburn	28	12	8	8	42	30	44
QPR	30	12	8	10	41	36	44
Ipswich	30	10	14	6	37	33	44
Tottenham	30	12	8	10	39	41	44
Man City	30	12	7	11	43	34	43
Coventry	30	11	10	9	44	40	43
Arsenal	28	11	6	11	26	25	39
Southampton	31	10	9	12	38	39	39
Leeds	31	10	9	12	41	45	39
Chelsea	30	9	10	11	32	38	37
Liverpool	29	9	9	11	39	40	36
Wimbledon	30	9	9	12	35	37	36
C Palace	30	8	10	12	36	46	34
Everton	30	9	6	15	33	41	33
Nottm Forest	29	8	7	14	29	38	31
Sheff Utd	30	8	7	15	31	41	31
Middlesbrough	30	7	9	14	37	52	30
Oldham	30	7	7	16	40	55	28

April 5

NORWICH 1

MANCHESTER UNITED 3

(Half-time score: 0-3)

Norwich: Gunn, Culverhouse, Polston, Sutton, Bowen, Goss, Crook, Megson (Ekoku 57), Phillips, Fox, Robins. Subs: Power, Walton
Scorer: Robins 61
Booked: Megson
United: Schmeichel, Parker, Bruce, Pallister, Irwin, McClair, Cantona, Ince, Kanchelskis (Robson 73), Giggs, Sharpe. Subs: Dublin, Sealey
Scorers: Giggs 13, Kanchelskis 20, Cantona 21
Booked: Robson, Ince
Referee: A Ward (London)
Attendance: 20,582
Weather: Fine

Manchester United showed all their class to move within a point of Aston Villa at the top of the Premier League. In the outstanding match of the season at Carrow Road they played football described by manager Alex Ferguson as "a breath of fresh air."

Ferguson was a delighted man after a performance rich in skill, style and stunning finishing. He said: "After the pain of last year I told the players to go out and enjoy it. I said that if we win our last seven games we would be champions as far as I'm concerned.

"We might, or might not, win the title but at the moment it doesn't matter. Whatever happens we will know we have given it a good crack. It was a marvellous performance but we have benefitted from having a 10-day break. There was a freshness about the side. it was like starting a new season."

Three goals in nine minutes from Giggs, Kanchelskis and Cantona buried Norwich's hope of killing off United's challenge. Their manager, Mike Walker, said: "Three goals in nine minutes is hard to swallow for any team. Give United credit. They had to come here and win and they did it. But we are not out of the thing yet."

Giggs' goal was created by Cantona, whose incisive pass split the Norwich defence leaving the young Welshman to skip past the goalkeeper Bryan Gunn and steer the ball into the net.

The second had its roots back in United's own penalty area. Gary Pallister broke up a Norwich attack before clearing to Brian McClair midway in his own half. McClair spotted Kanchelskis on the right wing and threaded the perfect ball along the touchline for the Ukrainian to race half the length of the pitch before beating Gunn at the near post.

Norwich were reeling on the ropes and United were not long in delivering the knockout blow. Paul Ince set up the killer punch, winning a crucial tackle on the halfway line and then beating three defenders on a driving run for the penalty area where he slipped the ball wide to Cantona. The Frenchman drove the ball high into the net off the post and Norwich were on their knees.

The Canaries fluttered briefly in the second half when Mark Robins, sold to Norwich by United in the close season, headed past Peter Schmeichel. But Fergie's men never looked in any real danger.

Kanchelskis races through to slot his shot past Norwich goalkeeper Bryan Gunn.

The swaggering Cantona was United's inspiration, and Ferguson said: "He was quite marvellous. The only difference from some of our recent matches was that we took our chances. We should have scored a few more."

But there was a shock the day after the match when United announced that Kanchelskis would be allowed to leave the club in the summer. Kanchelskis, frustrated at not being able to command a regular place in the side, started against Norwich only because Mark Hughes was suspended. He was replaced 18 minutes from time by Bryan Robson and left the pitch shaking his head.

Ferguson had some sympathy for the 24-year-old winger, who had also asked for a transfer earlier in the season, and told him he would not be held to the final year of his contract. Kanchelskis, on offer at around £1 million, said he would prefer to sign for another English club.

League Table After Match

	P	W	D	L	F	A	Pts
MAN UTD	36	18	12	6	54	28	66
Aston Villa	36	19	10	7	52	33	67
Norwich	37	19	8	10	51	52	65
Blackburn	34	14	11	9	51	34	53
Man City	35	14	8	13	49	40	50
Sheff Wed.	33	13	11	9	42	37	50
Coventry	37	13	11	13	48	47	50
QPR	36	13	10	13	48	46	49
Chelsea	36	12	13	11	42	42	49
Tottenham	34	13	10	11	43	49	49
Arsenal	33	13	8	12	33	30	47
Wimbledon	36	12	10	14	46	47	46
Liverpool	36	12	10	13	46	48	46
Southampton	37	12	10	15	48	51	46
Everton	36	13	6	17	43	45	45
Ipswich	36	10	15	11	41	45	45
Leeds	34	11	11	12	44	47	44
C. Palace	35	9	14	12	41	50	41
Oldham	35	10	8	17	52	62	38
Sheff Utd	34	10	7	17	40	44	37
Nottm Forest	35	9	9	17	33	48	36
Middlesbrough	36	8	10	18	42	64	34

April 10

Steve Bruce headed two late, late goals – one some seven minutes into injury time – to send Old Trafford into raptures. But it was Bryan Robson, United's original Captain Courageous, who earned the bulk of the praise from Alex Ferguson after the most improbable of victories. Bryan Robson, at 36, had had his appearances rationed by a series of injuries. But just when it seemed there was life after Bryan, he reappeared like a consultant surgeon waving his tray of instruments. A scalpel here and a stitch there and United, looking dead and gone, were suddenly leaping around the theatre.

Robson, who had been patrolling the touchline like an expectant father, was pushed on as substitute as soon as John Sheridan had stroked home the penalty that put Sheffield Wednesday in front. "When he did go on he started a decent passing game in the period of the game that was important," said Ferguson. "I was tinkering with that change before the goal went in. So when it did I had to bring him on straight away and it worked for us. It is going to be hard to leave him out of the side on Monday. He's already told me I have to play him or I'm off my head. He brought us a sense of purpose and nerve, too. He wanted to take the ball and to get involved all the time. His passing improved our team."

Robson has had his detractors during a celebrated career but few have questioned his influence, authority or valour. They were the qualities Ron Atkinson recognised at the very earliest age and which he fed and fostered at West Brom and then paid £1.5 million for as long ago as 1981. The Villa manager was certainly not doing handstands at this return. Among the ranks of the United players, Robbo is treated with reverence that borders on idolatry. His influence around the dressing room in the remaining days of this season would be critical.

Sheffield Wednesday, who have haunted United over the years, had been the last side Fergie wanted at this stage in proceedings. "Our record against them is bloody awful," said the United manager. "If there was one team we didn't want it was them, going into two cup finals and confident as well. We have come over a massive hurdle today."

COME ON BOYS …
Bryan Robson drives
United forward.

Some of that apprehension had clearly pervaded the side, and Wednesday boss Francis suggested: "You would have thought after Norwich they would have totally relaxed. But we sensed from the start the pressure was on them to go and win the League."

It was almost impossible for Fergie to appear laid-back as his talented forwards over-elaborated in the face of exemplary defending from Carlton Palmer and Viv Anderson.

"They were being far too clever," agreed Ferguson. "But sometimes when you have creative players you have to live with them. They were the same in the second-half at Norwich. They started getting careless.

"When they are precise, when they make the passes simple, then they are good enough to play like that. If we had got the early first goal as we should have, then we could have gone on to perform and score a few."

As it was, the carelessness became frustration and led to anxiety after Paul Ince had brought down the magnificent Chris Waddle for the penalty.

Bruce's two goals may well determine the destiny of the title. He said: "If that is the case I will look back on it as the highlight of my life. But we all showed great spirit and we kept coming back when the odds seemed stacked against us." Wednesday manager Francis, in a statement more of surprise than complaint, clocked Bruce's winner at "seven minutes and 14 seconds into injury time."

League Table After Match

	P	W	D	L	F	A	Pts
MAN UTD	37	19	12	6	56	29	69
Aston Villa	37	19	11	7	52	33	68
Norwich	38	15	11	10	52	57	65
Blackburn	36	15	11	10	56	40	56
QPR	37	14	10	13	52	49	52
Tottenham	35	14	10	11	48	50	52
Man City	36	14	9	13	50	41	52
Sheff Wed	35	13	12	10	44	40	51
Coventry	38	13	12	13	48	47	51
Arsenal	35	14	8	13	35	32	50
Chelsea	38	12	14	12	43	44	50
Wimbledon	37	13	10	14	50	47	49
Liverpool	36	13	10	13	47	48	49
Southampton	38	13	10	15	49	51	49
Everton	37	14	6	17	45	46	48
Leeds	36	14	6	17	45	46	48
Ipswich	38	10	16	12	43	48	46
Sheff Utd	38	11	8	17	43	46	41
C. Palace	36	9	14	13	41	54	41
Oldham	37	10	9	18	53	64	39
Middlesbrough	38	9	10	19	44	66	37
Nottm Forest	37	9	9	19	37	55	36

April 12

COVENTRY 0

MANCHESTER UNITED 1

(Half-time score: 0-1)

Coventry: Gould, Borrows, Atherton, Babb, McGrath (Jenkinson 71), Williams, Rennie, Hurst, Gynn, Wegerle, Quinn. Subs: Busst, Ogrizovic

Booked: Quinn, Borrows, Williams

Sent Off: Quinn

United: Schmeichel, Parker, Bruce, Pallister, Irwin, Giggs, Cantona (Robson 75), Ince, McClair, Sharpe. Hughes. Subs: Phelan, Sealey

Scorer: Irwin 40

Referee: R Gifford (Mid-Glamorgan)

Attendance: 24,429

Weather: Fine

Coventry were still smarting from the 5-0 drubbing they received earlier in the season at Old Trafford when United arrived at Highfield Road for the Easter Monday return. The points went home with United but the events on the ball were a sideshow compared to those off it.

The storm began to brew a few minutes from the end when Coventry's Mick Quinn appeared to push Peter Schmeichel and the giant United goalkeeper slumped to the ground. Referee Roger Gifford, who had his back to the incident, took the evidence of a linesman before ordering off Quinn, who had earlier been shown the yellow card following an incident with Steve Bruce. Furious Coventry players lambasted Peter Schmeichel for his part in the affair. New signing Roy Wegerle claimed: "Schmeichel took a dive. He faked it. Mick Quinn put his arms out trying to stop himself going forward. I saw it. I was a witness. I would go to any personal hearing on his behalf."

Danish international Schmeichel hit back. He said: "What Wegerle is saying is rubbish. I didn't go down on purpose. I'm a big man and it takes a lot to push me over. Quinn caught me by surprise when he shoved me. I wasn't expecting it and that's what sent me down. England is not like Italy and Spain where these things happen, and I know that. It doesn't happen here."

Quinn would only say: "I have been told to keep quiet and that's what I am going to do. Everyone saw what happened, they can form their own opinion. I have mine. The only judgement that matters to me is the one my manager makes. I will take any punishment on the chin."

Schmeichel, who had been a magnificent servant during the season, was suddenly to find himself engulfed in controversy and under a cloud of suspicion at a time when United could do without any distractions. The FA came down heavily on Spurs' Gordon Durie after he allegedly feigned injury in a clash with the same side earlier in the season. Durie was cleared on appeal. Now the fear was Schmeichel could also be in the dock. Days later, in a dramatic U-turn, referee Gifford admitted he had made a mistake in dismissing Quinn.

His late night review of the incident on BBC's Sportsnight had served to change his mind. Thankfully for United, the official took the view that though Schmeichel wasn't hurt he fell because he was genuinely surprised by the push.

So Schmeichel returned from World Cup duty in Latvia relieved to be in the clear – and United just four games away from their target. Bryan Robson had made a 15-minute appearance as substitute at Highfield Road, his 10th match of the season. After United's run of only two Premier League defeats in 23 games the chances of him making a full return were slight.

Fergie's reason for not bringing back Robbo was to make use of the width provided by Lee Sharpe and Ryan Giggs. United knew they had to succeed where Villa failed and open up Coventry to make any kind of game of it. The goal came, just as Ferguson suspected, through one of his wingers, Lee Sharpe. It was a simple affair. Sharpe, allowed space, played an easy ball a few feet inside for fullback Denis Irwin to come forward and drive his fourth goal of the season just inside the post.

All the attributes that had served Coventry in their draw at Villa Park were missing for only a couple of minutes, but United took full advantage.

Irwin salutes his winning goal.

League Table After Match

	P	W	D	L	F	A	Pts
MAN UTD	38	20	12	6	57	29	72
Aston Villa	38	20	11	7	53	33	71
Norwich	38	19	8	11	52	57	65
Blackburn	37	16	11	10	58	41	59
QPR	38	15	10	13	57	52	55
Sheff Wed.	36	14	12	10	49	42	54
Chelsea	39	13	14	12	47	46	53
Man City	37	14	10	13	51	42	53
Tottenham	36	14	19	12	49	52	52
Coventry	39	13	12	14	48	48	51
Arsenal	36	14	8	14	35	33	50
Liverpool	37	13	11	13	48	49	50
Wimbledon	38	13	10	15	52	51	49
Southampton	39	13	10	16	51	56	49
Everton	38	14	6	18	48	51	48
Leeds	36	12	11	13	50	51	47
Ipswich	39	10	16	13	44	50	46
C. Palace	37	10	14	13	45	55	44
Sheff Utd	38	11	8	17	43	46	41
Oldham	37	10	9	18	53	64	39
Nottm Forest	38	10	9	19	39	56	39
Middlesbrough	39	9	10	20	45	70	37

April 17

MANCHESTER UNITED 3

CHELSEA 0

(Half-time score: 2-0)

United: Schmeichel, Parker, Irwin, Bruce, Sharpe, Pallister, Cantona, Ince, McClair (Robson 49), Hughes, Giggs (Kanchelskis 68). Sub: Sealey

Scorers: Hughes 23, Clarke 44 (og), Cantona 48

Chelsea: Beasant, Clarke, Sinclair, Townsend, Johnsen, Donaghy (Barnard 69), Stuart, Spencer, Shipperley (Livingstone 55), Hall, Wise. Sub: Kharin

Referee: H King (Merthyr Tydfil)

Attendance: 40,139

Weather: Warm and sunny

The one thing no side could afford to do with Manchester United as they surged into top gear in the title run-in was to give them free hand-outs. When Chelsea came to Old Trafford Dave Beasant arrived with his giant hands full of gifts in the form of goalkeeping clangers.

Beasant, who had been exiled on loan to Grimsby, had only won his place back in the Chelsea team following manager Ian Porterfield's sacking. Porterfield had insisted Beasant would not play again for Chelsea because of a series of major errors but new boss Dave Webb had decided to give him another chance.

Webb must have wondered about the wisdom of that move after watching Mark Hughes's slightly mis-hit shot slip through Beasant's hands. Even Hughes admitted: "I was surprised when it went in. I didn't strike it well. I think Dave thought I was going to cross the ball."

United gratefully accepted the opportunity, however, and there was even more generosity to come in the form of a crazy own-goal by Chelsea defender Steve Clarke.

Lee Sharpe ran the ball down the right-hand side and checked before swinging in a left-foot cross into the heart of the Chelsea goalmouth. Eric Cantona was motoring to the far post but before the ball arrived Clarke raced into the gap in front of Cantona, wrong-footed Beasant and sent his header curling inside the far post.

It was 2-0, and when Cantona increased the lead just after half-time the pressure was off and United began to coast in the knowledge that they were about to go four points clear in the title race. It was only United's second victory over Chelsea at Old Trafford since 1966, and manager Alex Ferguson singled out Lee Sharpe for particular praise, saying he had been involved in 18 goals since his return from serious injury. "That," said Ferguson, "is a good contribution by any standards."

One intriguing insight to come out of the game was the developing relationship between Cantona and Hughes, who revealed they had developed a sign language which involved curious gesticulations and barely any dialogue.

"Last year I was up there on my own," Hughes explained. "Eric

has taken a lot of the weight off me. He likes to receive the ball like I do so we can take it in turns and share the workload." How do the two of them communicate? "Well, it's nods and winks and a bit of arm waving," said Hughes. "I enjoy playing with Eric. He is always looking to thread things into me in good areas on the edge of the box. He also enjoys knocking one-twos and when they come off, as they often do with him, the crowd love it. For me it is a joy to play in this side. The difference this time last year was that we were going into matches dreading them. Everything was a battle and a worry.

"We might have appeared confident but deep down we weren't really. Perhaps we felt there were underlying things wrong with our game and that they would be found out. Now we are confident in what we are doing. We have a lot of flair and a lot of pace right through the team and we can score from all departments. The criticism last season was at the end we ran out of goals. That won't happen this time. I think we are as confident as it is possible to be in football."

Cantona roars in to crash home the third.

League Table After Match

	P	W	D	L	F	A	Pts
MAN UTD	39	21	12	6	60	29	75
Aston Villa	38	20	11	7	53	33	71
Norwich	39	20	8	11	56	59	68
Blackburn	38	17	11	10	61	42	62
QPR	38	15	10	13	57	52	55
Tottenham	37	15	10	12	53	53	55
Sheff Wed	36	14	12	10	49	42	54
Liverpool	38	14	11	13	52	49	53
Chelsea	40	13	14	13	47	49	53
Man City	37	14	10	13	51	42	53
Wimbledon	39	14	10	15	53	51	52
Coventry	40	13	12	15	48	52	51
Arsenal	36	14	8	14	35	33	50
Southampton	40	13	11	16	51	56	50
Everton	39	14	7	18	48	51	49
Leeds	38	12	12	14	52	55	48
Ipswich	39	10	16	13	44	50	46
C. Palace	38	10	15	13	45	55	45
Sheff Utd	38	11	8	17	43	46	41
Oldham	39	10	10	19	55	69	40
Nottm Forest	39	10	9	20	39	57	39
Middlesbrough	39	9	10	20	45	70	37

April 21

CRYSTAL PALACE 0

MANCHESTER UNITED 2

(Half-time score: 0-0)

Palace: Martyn, Humphrey, Thorn, McGoldrick, Young, Shaw, Southgate, Newman, Osborn (Ndah 76), Armstrong, Coleman. Subs: Williams, Woodman

United: Schmeichel, Parker, Bruce, Pallister, Irwin, Kanchelskis (Robson 63), Ince, McClair, Giggs, Hughes, Cantona. Subs: Phelan, Sealey

Scorers: Hughes 64, Ince 89

Booked: Bruce

Referee: K Barratt (Coventry)

Attendance: 30,115

Weather: Fine

Mark Hughes claimed his 100th League goal for Manchester United to ignite some emotional celebrations at Selhurst Park. Once Hughes had struck in the 64th minute it was always going to be United's game.

Paul Ince's late contribution was memorable, and a parting gesture at the few remaining who doubted United were Championship material. It was a night which was to have a vital bearing on the title with Aston Villa losing 3-0 at Blackburn Rovers. United's fans accounted for more than half of the capacity 30,000 crowd and, with 15,000 watching on closed circuit at Old Trafford, the tension was initially reflected in the players. Palace, desperately battling against relegation, caused alarm in United's defence. They could have easily snatched a point but their strikeforce could not find sufficient penetration.

United's cosmopolitan mixture eventually surfaced for the vital goals. Hughes and Ince provided the final impact but Eric Cantona was the provider for both strikes. Cantona's craft and vision penetrated a Palace defence that had used Irish international Eddie McGoldrick as a sweeper. Cantona's cross was met by a characteristic volley from Hughes to record his 16th goal of the season. As the minutes ticked away for Ferguson it was Cantona again who provided him with relief when he sent Ince galloping on to goal. Ince, fulfilling all his potential in the heat of the title race, unleashed a drive of perfect accuracy and power into the far corner.

Palace's near-misses and goalmouth scrambles would soon be forgotten, but they nearly changed the course of events. None was more crucial than when, during a patchy first half, goalkeeper Peter Schmeichel made the first of two mistakes. On the half-hour he threw the ball quickly out to an unprepared Ryan Giggs, who was robbed by Eric Young. He gave Gareth Southgate possession and his neat through-ball was hit first time by Chris Armstrong only for the shot to clip the foot of the post. Ten minutes from the end, with Hughes' goal still not decisive, Schmeichel failed to hold an effort from Chris Coleman and presented Armstrong with a gift-wrapped opportunity. But he screwed the ball wide of the open goal.

Andrei Kanchelskis, replacing 'flu victim Lee Sharpe, had earlier given Brian McClair a clear shot which was fractionally wide. Giggs and McClair then both came close as United surged forward in search of the second goal. Despite a run of 24 points from a possible 33 United had been troubled often by Palace's determination. As Ferguson admitted: "They created a bit of panic for us from free-kicks and corners. It was typical of them." A confident Hughes said of his 100th goal: "It was probably the most significant goal I've scored and I can't see anybody stopping us now."

JUST FOR KICKS …
(Right) Hughes on the mark again.

League Table After Match

	P	W	D	L	F	A	Pts
MAN UTD	40	22	12	6	62	29	78
Aston Villa	40	21	11	8	56	37	74
Norwich	40	20	8	12	57	62	68
Blackburn	39	18	11	10	64	42	65
Liverpool	39	15	11	13	54	49	56
Sheff Wed	37	14	13	10	50	43	55
QPR	38	15	10	13	57	52	55
Tottenham	38	15	10	13	53	56	55
Man City	39	14	11	14	53	46	53
Wimbledon	40	14	11	15	54	52	53
Chelsea	40	13	14	13	47	49	53
Arsenal	37	14	9	14	36	34	51
Coventry	40	13	12	15	48	52	51
Southampton	40	13	11	16	51	56	50
Everton	39	14	7	18	48	51	49
Ipswich	40	11	16	13	47	51	49
Leeds	39	12	12	15	52	57	48
C. Palace	39	10	15	14	45	57	45
Sheff Utd	39	11	10	18	46	51	43
Oldham	39	10	10	19	55	69	40
Nottm Forest	40	10	10	20	40	58	40
Middlesbrough	40	10	10	20	48	70	40

May 3

MANCHESTER UNITED 3

BLACKBURN 1

(Half-time score: 1-1)
United: Schmeichel, Parker,
Irwin, Bruce, Sharpe (Robson 40),
Pallister, Cantona, Ince, McClair
(Kanchelskis 81), Hughes, Giggs.
Sub: Sealey
Scorers: Giggs 21, Ince 60,
Pallister 90
Booked: Bruce, Ince
Blackburn: Mimms, Marker
(Cowans 70), Le Saux, Sherwood,
Hendry, Moran (Andersson 74),
Ripley, Atkins, Gallacher,
Newell, Wilcox. Sub: Talia
Scorer: Gallacher 8
Booked: Marker
Referee: J Borrett (Great
Yarmouth)
Attendance: 40,447
Weather: Fine

Ryan Giggs was not even born in the halcyon days when George Best signalled a Manchester United victory by teasing the opposition with a mocking flourish of his fabulous footwork. But the slender and supple teenage winger provided Old Trafford again with that brushstroke of genius as a postscript to a stunning Championship victory.

The visit of Blackburn Rovers had been rendered incidental to United's title ambitions by the stumble of Aston Villa against Oldham the day before, and what was to have been a contest became a celebration. For this was not so much a football match as a festival. They had crossed continents to be here, for the support this football club enjoys is not parochial. The world is their parish. Blackburn, however, did not arrive here in party dress. They came for work with their sleeves rolled up and a European place in their focus. And then they had the audacity to take the lead. They had been blessed too, by the decision of referee Jim Borrett, who had not given what on video looked a sure penalty when Paul Parker stuck out a leg for Jason Wilcox to fall over.

But United made sure they won it all the same. It would have been easy for them to take their foot off the accelerator. The chequered flag had already been passed. Instead they slipped smoothly into overdrive.

Up strode Giggs to arrow a free-kick over a defensive wall and into the top corner of the net as if it had been tracked there by computer. That explosive strike won an approving nod from Michel Platini, the master of the art of free-kick taking, sitting as a guest in the director's box. Not to be upstaged, Lee Sharpe then gave Blackburn goalkeeper Bobby Mimms the chance to exercise his back muscles as he bent to turn a fine shot over his crossbar.

Ferguson chose the half-time interval as the opportune moment to give Bryan Robson his share of the bubbling atmosphere. He might have responded with a goal but when Eric Cantona provided the chance Colin Hendry's body got in the way. So it was left to Paul Ince, who idolises Robbo, to show him the way, driving his angled shot past Mimms after Cantona had exquisitely provided the perfect pass. United still managed one last hurrah. They won a free-kick in

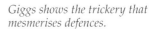
Giggs shows the trickery that mesmerises defences.

the final moments and called on Gary Pallister to take it.

He was the only United player not to have scored all season. And as if on cue he drove it low into the net. Neat and tidy.

Robson and Bruce then received the Premier League trophy and the way they had played, with wonderful imagination, even on Merseyside they might just have been prepared to concede that they were worthy champions.

League Table After Match

	P	W	D	L	F	A	Pts
MAN UTD	41	23	12	6	65	30	81
Aston Villa	41	21	11	9	56	38	74
Norwich	41	21	8	12	58	62	71
Blackburn	40	18	11	11	65	45	65
Man City	40	15	11	14	54	46	56
QPR	39	15	11	13	58	53	56
Liverpool	40	15	11	14	54	50	56
Chelsea	41	14	14	13	49	50	56
Tottenham	39	15	11	13	54	57	56
Sheff Wed.	38	14	13	11	52	46	55
Wimbledon	41	14	12	15	55	53	54
Arsenal	38	14	10	14	36	34	52
Coventry	41	13	12	16	49	54	51
Everton	40	14	8	18	48	51	50
Southampton	41	13	11	17	51	57	50
Leeds	40	12	13	15	53	58	49
Ipswich	41	11	16	14	48	54	49
C. Palace	40	11	15	14	48	58	48
Sheff Utd	40	12	10	18	48	51	46
Oldham	40	11	10	19	56	69	43
Middlesbrough	41	11	10	20	51	72	43
Nottm Forest	41	10	10	21	40	60	40

May 9

They rounded it off in tidy style with seven straight wins, a 10 point lead and a playing record identical to the heroes of 1967 whose ghosts they exorcised.

Yet you could not have blamed United if they had wanted the season to go on for ever. In the last few weeks they looked invincible.

It was Wimbledon's good fortune to be at home for United's final game. The crowd of 30,115, the biggest since 18,500 saw the Dons play HMS Victory in an amateur cup game in 1935, paid record receipts of £303,000.

The crowd were, in the main, those who had assembled from across the country to pay final homage to the new Premier League champions.

"We could have come and been carried away by the mood of the crowd. But we showed a winner's attitude. When there were 50-50 balls we won them," said Ferguson. "The performance was in keeping with the attitude of the whole team. I must say I've never been kissed so much in my life."

United saved their last goal of a glorious season for their distinguished skipper Bryan Robson. It was his first in the Premier League. "Gary Pallister threw down the challenge that after his goal in the game with Blackburn I was the only one who hadn't scored. So I had to get one," said Robson.

Wimbledon had not intended to sit out the party, and Vinnie Jones took only five seconds to post his notice of intent on Paul Ince's thigh, a tackle that later in the game might have been a sending-off offence. Wimbledon's style is the complete opposite of what we have grown to admire from United and it made for a fascinating and exciting contest. But the harder the tackles the more sophisticated became United's method of dealing with them.

The Frenchman's flicks and feints assured the ball was gone before the boot came in, perhaps tiring of the treatment, retribution was exacted on John Fashanu in one flowing movement. It earned a pat on the head from Vinnie. What this game also underlined was just how commanding and peerless Gary Pallister and Steve Bruce have become at the heart of United's defence. And it proved conclusive evidence of the exceptional progress made by Paul Ince, who scored for the third successive match to give United the lead. Ince ought to have put United in front after half an hour when Jones attempted a suicidal pass across the edge of his own area.

Lee Sharpe might have beaten Ince to the first goal just before halt-time when he drew Hans Segers into an exceptional flying save. Ryan Giggs, who started on the subs' bench to give Robson his chance, came on for the second-half as replacement for Denis Irwin, who pulled a thigh muscle. That generated the best from Cantona who showed some thrilling skills. He it was who headed out a Giggs corner in the 65th minute for Ince to volley home off the heel of Scott Fitzgerald.

Robson then timed his run on to Steve Bruce's chip with all his old precision to spring the offside trap and drive the ball home left-footed. Dean Holdsworth had the final word with an 82nd minute headed consolation goal from Warren Barton's cross for his 19th goal of the season.

Ferguson said: "It was fantastic for Robbo. I am really pleased for him." And so was Wimbledon manager Joe Kinnear, who said: "The most attractive side won the League. They played exceptionally well this season. They have shown today they have determination. They are solid through the side and I was pleased for Robson because he has been a magnificent professional."

It was a tribute that might well have been echoed across the country, and United showed just how comfortably the title of champions rests on their shoulders.

League Table After Match

	P	W	D	L	F	A	Pts
MAN UTD	42	24	12	6	67	31	84
Aston Villa	42	21	11	10	57	40	74
Norwich	42	21	9	12	61	65	72
Blackburn	42	20	11	11	68	46	71
QPR	41	16	12	13	60	54	60
Liverpool	42	16	11	15	62	55	59
Sheff Wed	41	15	14	12	54	48	59
Man City	42	15	12	15	56	51	57
Arsenal	41	15	11	15	39	35	56
Chelsea	42	14	14	14	51	54	56
Tottenham	41	15	11	15	57	65	56
Wimbledon	42	14	12	16	56	55	54
Everton	42	15	8	19	53	55	53
Sheff Utd	42	14	10	18	54	53	52
Coventry	42	13	13	16	52	57	52
Ipswich	42	12	16	14	50	55	52
Leeds	42	12	15	15	57	62	51
Southampton	42	13	11	18	54	61	50
Oldham	42	13	10	19	63	74	49
C. Palace	42	11	16	15	48	61	49
Middlesbrough	42	11	11	20	54	75	44
Nottm Forest	42	10	10	22	41	62	40

Pallister and Jones scrap it out.

Meet
the Champions

---

*Profile of the Premier
League Championship
Winners*

---

by

FRANK MALLEY

Peter Schmeichel

Every time Peter walks out on to the Old Trafford pitch he has to pinch himself to make sure it is all true. As a small boy Peter dreamed of playing for United. From his home in Gladsaxe, near Copenhagen, he was enchanted by the glamour of Charlton and Best and has been a fan all his life, with posters on his bedroom wall and a yearning to run out at Old Trafford in his heart. But when he signed for United, to replace the shattered nerves of Jim Leighton and stopgap keeper Les Sealey in a £750,000 deal from Brondby in August 1991, it was not all smooth going.

In one of his first games the giant goalkeeper, whose nickname is the Terminator because of his physical resemblance to film star Arnold Schwarzenegger, received a bruising buffeting from John Fashanu and the rest of the Crazy Gang at Wimbledon when they realised he was weak on high crosses. Alex Ferguson found the solution – ordering United's big men to pound in on Schmeichel in training as high balls were thrown into the penalty area. "You're not tested like that back home in Denmark and there are some goals I conceded which I don't look back on with any pride," said Schmeichel.

The improvement was swift and marked. Not that Schmeichel is always that busy in the United goal. He said: "It has been made a lot easier for me by the fact that I play behind such a great defence. Gary Pallister and Steve Bruce have given me great protection. I'm not joking when I say a dustbin could have kept goal for us in some games. The defence has been that good."

It is a far cry from his Danish First Division days when he played almost like a sweeper behind the Brondby defence and was famous for taking as well as saving penalties. He was named 1990 Danish Player of the Year and won his first cap for Denmark against Greece in June 1987. He made his League debut for United against Notts County on the opening day of the 1991-92 season and was an inspirational figure behind Denmark's European Championship success in 1992.

Denis Irwin

Denis is the quiet man of the United dressing room, which is surprising since he was born in the blarney-capital of Cork. His brilliant defending did all the talking necessary, however, when he was playing for his former club, Oldham, then of the Second Division, against United in the FA Cup semi-final in 1990. Alex Ferguson was so impressed with the way Irwin dealt with United's strikeforce that he signed him that summer for £625,000. Ferguson said: "He had been on our shortlist before but his performance against us in the Cup underlined his potential." That promise has blossomed at Old Trafford, and Irwin was capped by Republic of Ireland manager Jack Charlton against Morocco after just two games in a United shirt. At 5ft 7ins Irwin is a strong tackler who can play on either flank. He is quick to link up with the attack and has scored some memorable long-range goals with his powerful right foot. he also takes dangerous in-swinging corners but possibly his biggest asset is his temperament. "I'm not the worrying sort," he says.

NUMBER ONE …
Denis Irwin celebrates his first goal of the season.

129

Paul Parker

Paul's polished brand of defending helped England to reach the World Cup semi-finals in Italy in 1990. He was a pacy fullback with a spring in his step and a sackful of medals in his cabinet. All Paul's dreams seemed to have come true – than came his worst nightmare in a wintry midweek night match while playing for Queens Park Rangers a few months after returning from Italy. "I tore the cruciate ligament in my left knee," said Paul. "It was in a 'nothing' game, the Zenith Data at Southampton. But for an hour or so that night I thought I was finished, that I would never play again. I missed most of that season and will always be grateful to England manager Graham Taylor for taking me on the 1991 summer tour of Australia, New Zealand and Malaysia. I needed it to prove my fitness to the big clubs who wanted to sign me and it helped me land a move to Manchester United." Alex Ferguson splashed out £1.7 million for Paul, who forced his way back into the England side against West Germany at Wembley – when his injury jinx struck again. "I should have come off when I felt something in my hamstring, but was so naive I played on," said Paul. "It was a new injury to me and I did more damage than I thought." The problem kept him out of United's failed championship chase in 1992, the European Championships in Sweden and the first quarter of the title season, though when he did win back his place he was one of the first names on Ferguson's team sheet. "I don't believe I am injury prone, just unlucky," said Paul, who comes from Dagenham." The big problems are behind me. The knee is stronger than before the injury and the hamstring is fine." He is back as chirpy as ever in the Old Trafford dressing room where he is known as "Busby" after the bird who appeared in the British Telecom ads … because he is always on the 'phone.

Steve Bruce

Steve, a product of the famous Wallsend Boys' Club, has bravery written all over his face. Or to be more exact his nose, which he has broken six times in the job of keeping top class strikers at bay. United's team captain in Bryan Robson's absence, Steve was arguably United's most consistent player in 1992-93. He also holds the rather dubious honour of being United's only non-international, a fact which his team mates are always quick to point out in good-humoured fashion.

It's something with which Bruce has learned to come to terms. He said: "I bumped into former England manager Bobby Robson in Benfica. He came up to me and said "I should have capped you." It was nice to hear but it still doesn't get me one. I'm a great believer in what you've never had you never miss … and anyway, when they all clear off on international duty I get a nice few days off. I'll always be a little disappointed I didn't get one. I get some stick about it but it's good humoured and I'm big enough to take it."

Steve, in fact, is just happy to be playing in the Premier League after Newcastle, Sunderland and Sheffield Wednesday advised him as a teenager that he would never succeed as a professional. Incredibly, they didn't think he would be tough enough.

It looked as if he was on course for a plumbing job until he was taken on by Gillingham, and his first reaction to their enquiries was: "Where the hell is it." He eventually found out and stayed seven years before moving on to Norwich and then to United in 1987. "It was the biggest thrill of the lot to find out United wanted me. I needed a slap to make me realise it was true." Steve, who plays the odd game of golf and cricket for relaxation, is something of a prolific scorer for a defender, having scored 19 in the 1991-92 season – 11 of them from the penalty spot. He is married to childhood sweetheart Janet and has two children.

Gary Pallister

Gary signed for United for a club record £2.3m from Middlesbrough in August 1989 in one of the moves sanctioned during Michael Knighton's short reign at Old Trafford. That price tag was a far cry from the £60-a-week wages which Middlesbrough directors were reluctant to pay Pallister when he joined them from non-league Billingham Town in 1984. A local tycoon stepped in to guarantee his wages for four months. After a shaky start he showed his class as a dominant defender with lots of pace and comfortable playing the ball out of defence.

As former Middlesbrough boss Willie Maddren predicted: "He could become another Alan Hansen if his concentration improves." He was voted United's Player of the Year in his first season and also named Players' Player of the Year in 1991-92. He started his working life as a tea boy on an oil rig at 17 and his first love was cricket. He used to be a fast bowler for Junior League team Norton but Middlesbrough persuaded him to quit the summer game because it was giving him tendonitis. He is known as a bit of a prankster in the United dressing room, and scored his first goal of the Championship campaign with a free-kick in the last minute of the penultimate game against Blackburn. A full England international, he won his first cap against Hungary in April 1988.

Pallister leaps between Liverpool's Barnes and McManaman.

Paul Ince

Paul, a competitive midfield player who blossomed with United's growing success, was a self-confessed tearaway in his younger days. His dad left when he was a toddler. His mum later went to live in Germany when he was 11. Paul went to stay with relatives in London's tough East End. This wild lifestyle almost ruined his career as a junior at West Ham and he is always quick to acknowledge the debt he owes to former West Ham manager John Lyall, who supported him through some troubled times.

"I owe him so much," said Paul. "And had the Hammers not sacked him I might still have been at Upton Park." Not that Paul regrets moving to Old Trafford in 1989 – even though it was a transfer fraught with problems. The initial move was called off at the eleventh hour when a deep-seated groin injury was discovered at his medical. "Paul was in tears. I'd never seen him so upset," said his wife Clare, who went to the same Ilford school as Paul. "I just told him, "It's not the end of the world. I'll stick by you."

Happily a second opinion eased the concern, though United insisted on a reduced fee of £800,000 for him, with the added proviso that they would pay £8,000 per match over an agreed period. That looked increasingly like a bargain deal as his blend of tough tackling and creative skills earned him a regular place in England manager Graham Taylor's side. And Paul knows exactly what helped him to throw off the bad boy image which constantly found him in trouble with referees – his one-year-old son Thomas Christopher. "Before we had the baby, football was the be all and end all," he said. "I used to come home in a hump if we lost. Now I see Thomas smiling and it changes everything. There's only room for one baby in the house."

Paul made his United debut in a 5-1 League win over Millwall. He is a great friend of boxer Frank Bruno and a cousin of Nigel Benn, and one thing he hates is being dubbed "the new Bryan Robson." With his more mature outlook he would rather be known as the "new Paul Ince."

Lee Sharpe

The deal which took Lee to Old Trafford was thrashed out in a sleek Jaguar parked behind Torquay United's ground after a midweek night match. Alex Ferguson, who had watched the game disguised in a balaclava, was so impressed with Lee, a wiry 16-year-old YTS recruit at the time, that he vowed not to leave the ground until he had an agreement to buy. He sent a message to Torquay manager Cyril Knowles to meet him and his assistant Archie Knox in his car after the game and at 1.30 in the morning Torquay chairman Len Pope was called from his bed to conclude the deal. Lee cost just £60,000 down with further agreed payments and an exhibition match taking the completed transfer to £200,000. The deal however, was mutually beneficial saving Torquay from the threat of closure and providing United with a left-sided player with tremendous pace. In his early days at Old Trafford Lee was often used as a left back but his attacking career really took off after a brilliant hat-trick which helped beat Arsenal 6-2 in the Rumbelows Cup at Highbury in November 1990.

He won an England cap as a substitute in a European Championship game against the Republic of Ireland at Wembley in March 1991 and in the same month was awarded the PFA Young Player of the Year award. Then came the agony of a troublesome groin injury which refused to heal and, more worryingly, a bout of meningitis which kept him out of the game for the best part of a season. It was November 7 before Lee burst into action in United's title-winning season in the 1-0 defeat at Aston Villa, but after that his creative contribution was substantial. Lee comes from the Birmingham suburb of Halesowen and his younger brother John was an apprentice with Manchester City, after also having had trials at Old Trafford.

Brian McClair

Brian was Alex Ferguson's first major signing for United in the summer of 1987. One thing is certain, the Scotland striker and midfield man would have had no problems working out the intricacies of the £850,000 deal. Brian studied for a BSc in mathematics for two years at Glasgow University while playing part-time football with Motherwell in 1981-82 and then gave up the course when Celtic offered him a four-year contract. "I decided to give soccer a go," said Brian. "I knew I could always go back to university and may still do one day. A job as a maths teacher appeals to me and it is nice to have options." He signed for Celtic in 1983 after Charlie Nicholas had been sold to Arsenal, and in four years there scored 99 goals. In his first season with United "Chocky", as he is known to his team-mates, was top scorer with 31 goals, though his United career has alternated between midfield and attack. Like Eric Cantona, who had won the title with Leeds in 1992, McClair had already sampled something of the heady aroma of championship success in his teenage days at Aston Villa: "I was a first year apprentice at Villa when they won it in 1981," said McClair. "I swept the first team dressing room and cleaned captain Dennis Mortimer's boots. We were invited to the civic reception and it was great to feel part of the club's success." He was certainly an integral part of United's triumph, a particular highlight being his two goals against Sheffield Wednesday which earned a vital championship point on Boxing Day. Music is Brian's passion away from football and he is a rock and pop expert, often to be found immersed in an impromptu quiz with Alex Ferguson on the team coach. Brian, who lists Billy Bragg and the Pogues as his favourite musicians, is usually victorious. He also loves video games and playing with his home computer, and as you might expect from a university boffin his favourite TV programme is Inspector Morse. He lives with his wife Maureen and three children in Cheshire and has just one more aim: "To stay at United until the end of my playing career. And, of course, to win another title."

Eric Cantona

Alex Ferguson describes Eric, with some understatement, as his "most opportune" signing. Others would say the £1.2 million Ferguson paid Leeds for the highly talented French international in November 1992 has turned into the footballing bargain of the decade. With his deft touches he added immense and immediate variety to United's attacking options and scored four crucial goals in his first six league games. Both Ferguson and Leeds manager Howard Wilkinson have applauded his temperament and his "fantastic attitude" to training even though he came to England with a bit of a wild man reputation. At 26, he has seen service with Auxerre (twice) Marigues, Marseille (twice) Bordeaux, Montpellier, Nimes and Sheffield Wednesday, as well as Leeds and United. His tastes are more highbrow than your average English League player and he relaxes by painting, writing poetry or walking in the country. Eric met his wife Isabelle, 30, when she was a 20-year-old student of philosophy and language at university in Aix-en-Provence and he was a 17-year-old apprentice at a college for football skills. They have been married six years, have a four-year-old son Raphael and have settled in the outskirts of Leeds, near to the great sweep of the North Yorkshire moors. Team-mates and opponents alike cannot praise him enough. David Burrows, the Liverpool defender who Cantona took apart when scoring a Charity Shield hat-trick in Leeds' 4-3 victory over Liverpool in 1992, said: "Cantona has a vast amount of flair and quality and an eye for goal. I couldn't get near him that day. If you give an international player like him a lot of space he's going to show his quality and he did. He does things off the cuff and when they come off he looks really good. If they don't he doesn't let it worry him too much."

Mark Hughes

Mark, at 5ft 8in and 12 stone, is not exactly a big man but his physical presence is virtually unrivalled in the game. That's why he is called "Thunder Thighs" and there are plenty of defenders who could testify to his remarkable strength. Mark has a reputation for being a difficult striker to play with and his special brand of shielding the ball perplexed Brian McClair for at least two seasons. It took the arrival of Eric Cantona, with his extra vision and flair, to really get the best out of Wrexham-born Mark.

He chalked up his 100th League goal for United in the 2-0 win at Crystal Palace – and that's a feat accomplished by just nine other United players, including Bobby Charlton (199), Denis Law (171) and George Best (137). 'Sparky' made his United debut in 1983 and made 89 League appearances before moving to Barcelona to play for Terry Venables. Hughes signed an eight-year deal with the Spanish club but was too young and inexperienced to produce his best form in front of 90,000 fanatic fans. He quickly found himself on loan to Bayern Munich, a period he enjoyed. "When I left United my style was a bit over-physical and my aggression in Spain got me into trouble, even when I didn't do anything wrong." said Hughes. "I was only half the player I had been in England. I enjoyed myself in Germany and will always be grateful to Uli Hoeness for getting my game back on the rails."

Mark returned to United in June 1988 and has twice won the PFA Player of the Year award. He scored two goals in the 3-3 FA Cup Final against Crystal Palace in 1990 which United went on to win in a replay. And he won the European Cup Winners' Cup for United with a magnificent strike, ironically against Barcelona, a year later.

He lives with wife Jill and their three children in the Cheshire village of Prestbury but has never lost touch with his roots and often returns for a drink with his pals at the Duke of Wellington pub at Ruabon. He gained six O-levels and once thought of going on to further studies … until, that is a Manchester United scout knocked on his door.

Ryan Giggs

If Ryan had £1 for every time he has been hailed as the "new George Best" he could have financed the rebuilding of the Stretford End all by himself. It is a measure of his sublime skill that the comparison has gathered more credence with each passing month. He is simply the most exciting talent in the English game, possessing tremendous pace, superb balance and wonderful individual skills. Yet despite all the hype that has accompanied his rise to fame since he made his League debut, aged just 17, as a substitute for Denis Irwin against Everton at Old Trafford in March 1991, he has remained remarkably calm. Ryan lives at home with his mum, has a steady girlfriend, and a manager in Alex Ferguson who has protected him from distractions – like agents, sponsorship deals and the media. That, Ryan reckons, is one of the big differences between Best and himself. He said: "I have a steady family life whereas George came over at 15 from Belfast by himself. He didn't have as many minders as I've got. I just try to lead a quiet life. You have to be careful where you go and what you do. I've been warned about that by the manager. But my mum's with me and I think I can handle it. I'm happy living at home. It keeps my feet on the ground and helps me live a normal existence. Getting noticed in the street has come as a big shock but it's something I've enjoyed. I don't think I'm anything like George Best apart from my age and the fact I play for United. Best was a great player and hopefully one day I can be as good as him." By the age of 19 Cardiff-born Ryan had twice been voted young player of the year by the PFA which shows the regard his fellow professionals held for his talent. He struck some exceptional goals in the race for the title and also scored a superb 25-yard free-kick goal in his first full international for Wales against Belgium, after which veteran Welsh defender Kevin Ratcliffe said: "Now I can tell my grandchildren I've played with Ryan Giggs." There could be no finer compliment.

Bryan Robson

Bryan, or Captain Marvel as he is affectionately known throughout soccer, was presented with an honorary Bachelor of Arts degree by Manchester University in 1992. A degree in medical science might have been more appropriate considering the amount of time Bryan has spent in hospital operating theatres during his 36 years. His career was threatened by broken legs while a youngster with West Brom and his 1986 World Cup in Mexico with England was wrecked by a constantly dislocating shoulder. He has had an achilles tendon operation, been involved in a tongue swallowing scare and had prolonged spells out with ankle, groin, hamstring and thigh injuries. On top of those a damaged sciatica nerve kept him sidelined for most of the championship winning season and almost deprived him of a League Championship medal. But you won't find United's greatest player of the last 10 years complaining about having to sit it out on the subs bench. "The lads played so well that there was no way the boss could change the line-up" said Bryan, who was born in Chester Le Street on 11 January 1957. "When I was a child, I was taken to see United in a cup tie when the team included Law, Best and Charlton. That day I decided the only club to follow was United. It was one of the greatest days of my life when I signed." Despite Robbo's lengthy list of injuries he won 90 caps for England, scoring 26 goals, which included a hat-trick in the 8-0 destruction of Turkey in 1984. With a greetings card business and other interests he no longer needs to play for money and admits he drives himself through long fitness battles because of the "sheer enjoyment" of being a footballer. He lives in a five bedroomed detached house in Cheshire with wife Denise and their three children, Claire, Charlotte and Ben. His youngest brother Gary, 27, plays for West Brom while his other brother Justin had to quit Newcastle United because of injury. Bryan, a big racing fan, owns his own racehorse, drives a Mercedes and also enjoys golf. He loves relaxing by watching *Cheers* and *Coronation Street*. His favourite sportsman outside soccer is Spanish golf star Seve Ballesteros. "He has a great temperament," said Robbo. Many would say they are two of a kind – born winners.

Andrei Kanchelskis

The championship winning season was tinged with a personal family tragedy. Andrei, a fast-raiding winger from the Ukraine, pulled out of the FA Cup fourth round clash with Brighton in January. Andrei spent much of the rest of the season sitting on the substitute's bench, struggling to retain a regular first team place after the return of Lee Sharpe from injury and illness. Whenever he got into action, however, he was a firm favourite with the Old Trafford crowd with his thrilling runs and occasional spectacular goal. He joined United in May 1991 for £1m from Shaktyor Donetsk.

Clayton Blackmore

A versatile player who can operate in midfield or defence. Has found it difficult to hold down a regular first team place at Old Trafford in the title season after signing apprentice forms for United in May 1981. A full Welsh international, he made his debut for United in May 1984 against Nottingham Forest. Possesses a powerful shot and is dangerous at free-kicks. Collected an FA Cup medal against Crystal Palace in 1990 and was also in the side which won the European Cup Winners' Cup in 1991.

Mike Phelan

Mike served his apprenticeship with Burnley before moving on to Norwich in July 1985. He captained the Canaries during their successful 1988-89 season. He is another versatile player who can operate in midfield, at fullback or in the middle of defence. He ended the 89-90 season as the only player to appear in all United's 38 League matches. Has good pace and reads the game well.

Dion Dublin

A big, powerful striker, he had a brief spell at Norwich as a youngster before joining Cambridge. Moved to Old Trafford for £1 million but broke a leg against Crystal Palace in only his sixth appearance. Returned to full fitness after a six-month lay-off as substitute for Andrei Kanchelskis against Oldham on March 9, 1993, but struggled to maintain a first-team place.

Darren Ferguson

There is always an added pressure being the manager's son and playing in the first team. Just ask Brian Clough's son, Nigel, at Nottingham Forest. Midfield man Darren, however, coped admirably as he progressed through Old Trafford's junior ranks and he kept Neil Webb out of the United team at the beginning of the 1992 season. Alex Ferguson's other two sons opted for careers in education, but Darren only ever wanted to be a footballer. Alex said: "As a footballer he went to Spurs and Nottingham Forest for trials and Brian Clough wanted to sign him. He made a terrific offer to the lad. But when I moved from Aberdeen to manager United there was only one place Darren wanted to be and that was Old Trafford. I was naturally a bit cautious about signing him because I know the pressures that a manager's son can face. But Archie Knox, then my assistant, and coach Brian Kidd said it would be silly to let a good player like him go to Forest. I am happy I made the decision I made."

Darren, who made his debut against Sheffield United in February 1991, was in the news for events other than football in the summer of 1992. He was mugged by armed robbers while on holiday in New Orleans with United teammate Kieran Toal. The pair handed over 40 dollars and the robbers let them go, shaken but unhurt, Darren said: "It was a nightmare. We won't be going back to New Orleans in a hurry."

Alex Ferguson

Manchester United Chairman Martin Edwards did not waste any time following Ron Atkinson's departure in November 1986. He knew who he wanted and he caught the first plane to Aberdeen to sign Ferguson, a man who was fast building a reputation as the best manager in Britain, after collecting major honours in eight years in Scotland. Six years and several months later Ferguson, a self-confessed workaholic, had rebuilt the club sufficiently to hand over the Premier League title, and with that he became the first man to adequately fill the manager's chair at Old Trafford, since the retirement of Sir Matt Busby. Born in Govan, Glasgow on New Year's Eve, 1941, Ferguson is the son of a Clyde shipyard worker. He made his Scottish League debut as a player for Queen's Park in 1957 and had spells with St Johnstone and Dunfermline. In 1967 he signed for Rangers and also played for Falkirk and Ayr. He once ran a pub in Glasgow called Fergie's Bar before going into management with East Stirling. It is easy to recite the cold facts, not so easy to get close to a man with a granite exterior. *Daily Express* chief soccer writer Steve Curry, who knows Fergie well said: "Ferguson is an intense man whose moods can be gauged by a look into his pale blue eyes. You can find exceptional warmth and generosity there; humour too. But they can darken into pools of anger and woe betide those who cross him. His outbursts have become part of club folklore, withering explosions when he feels his own honesty has been abused or the club's name besmirched." Many a pressman has been on the receiving end of the most cutting tongue in soccer. Many an errant footballer too. Ferguson received the OBE for services to soccer and took over the Scotland manager's job on a temporary basis following Jock Stein's death during the World Cup qualifiers in 1986. He turned down the permanent job and Scotland's loss was United's gain. Under Ferguson United have won the FA Cup (1990), the European Cup Winners' Cup (1991), the European Super Cup (1991) and the Football League Cup (1992) as well as the first Premier League Trophy (1993). Ferguson is married with three grown-up sons.

Where are they now?

Profile of United's 1967
First Division
Winners

They were called the Class of '67 and most Manchester United fans can recite their names as if they formed a nursery rhyme. But what happened to those heroes of the Beatles era?

As they pay their tribute to the new champions we remember their days of glory.

by
STEVE CURRY

Alex Stepney

Born Mitcham, 18.9.44. Games 535. Goals 2. Honours: League Championship 66/67; European Cup 67/68; FA Cup 76/77. 1 England cap.

Stepney made 35 appearances in the Championship season. He now works as the manager of a car rental company and still does some scouting on behalf of his old pal Alan Ball at Exeter City. When Sir Matt bought Stepney for a then record £55,000 from Chelsea at the start of the Championship season, he was almost completing the jigsaw. Harry Gregg, a Munich survivor, was the victim of career-ending injuries and Busby felt that the Londoner would be his ideal replacement.

Stepney had made his name in the early Sixties with Millwall where he played 137 matches before moving on to Chelsea. But he played only one match for the Stamford Bridge club before Busby made his plunge. He was to play a significant part in winning the title, and an even more important one in securing the European Cup the following season. One save against Eusebio towards the end of normal time against Benfica guaranteed his immortality among Manchester United supporters.

Alex was to spend 12 years at Old Trafford, unlucky that his best years coincided with those of Ray Clemence and Peter Shilton. He won only one cap for England, in the game against Sweden in May 1968, which England won 3-1. Always renowned as a dressing room joker and five-a-side striker, Stepney remained proud of the two goals he scored – both penalties – for the club.

When his career with United came to a close in 1977-78, Stepney had a spell playing in America with the Dallas Tornadoes and with non-League Altrincham before taking up retirement. He said: "It is about time that Manchester United were the English champions again and I congratulate them. They should perhaps have done it the previous season but threw their chance away. But they seem to have learned their lesson. The signing of Paul Ince seemed to make a big difference. I don't believe anyone in football can say they didn't deserve it."

Tony Dunne

Born Dublin 24.7.41. Games 529. Goals 2. Honours: League Championship 64/65, 66/67. FA Cup 62/63; 33 Republic of Ireland caps.

Tony Dunne made 40 appearances in the Championship season. He now owns his own golf driving range in Altrincham. By common agreement Tony Dunne has been the best fullback Manchester United have produced over the last 30 years, and he is mentioned alongside Munich victim Roger Byrne as an outstanding defender. He was bought from Irish club Shalbourne for a mere £6,000 by Sir Matt Busby in 1960, and he was to be a fixture in the Manchester United sides for a decade.

His greatest asset was his pace, for he was short at 5ft 6ins and weighed just under 10 stone. But he had a rare tenacity that made him a formidable opponent. There was nothing complicated to Dunne's game. He had a simple win-it and give-it philosophy from which players like Paddy Crerand would benefit. Indeed, his critics would suggest that he didn't use his pace enough going forward, but Dunne was essentially a defender of high quality. He played more matches in the Championship side than any player other than George Best and Bobby Charlton.

It caused raised eyebrows when he was sold by Tommy Docherty to Bolton in 1973 because it was still felt by many fans that he had much to offer at Old Trafford. Indeed, he was to add a further 170 matches to his career total under Ian Greaves at Burnden Park, where he was successfully used late in his career as a sweeper. He said: "I can see a really successful run now for this Manchester United side. I believe the side I played in had just about everything. This one is not far short of that. Breaking the barrier has been achieved now and they could dominate the English scene. Apart from the skill they are organised. We were not a tactical side. We just played. We should have won more than we did."

Bobby Noble

Born Manchester 18.12.45. Games 33. Goals 0. Honours: League Championship 66/67.

Made 29 appearances in the League Championship side. Noble was regarded as perhaps the ideal build for a full-back. He had excellent balance and weight ratio, was lightning quick and had a tackle that was like a vice. He is the least remembered of the side, however, because his career was tragically curtailed by a car crash. He was just 21 at the time, had played 29 consecutive matches in the season and was in a car travelling back from a match at Roker Park. The injuries he sustained almost claimed his life but they certainly ended his career before it had a chance to really blossom. There were confident predictions that he would become a full England international, and Bobby has had to live down the years with the frustration of not knowing just how far in the game he might have developed.

He said: "I can only say how brilliant a side ours was to play in. There were never any instructions given. We were merely told to go out and express and enjoy ourselves. I don't go to Old Trafford now but I do watch the side when they are on television and things look very good for them. It has taken time for Alex Ferguson to build the side but now the title has been won I'm sure he will look to strengthen and I can only see it getting better."

Pat Crerand

Born Glasgow 19.2.39. Games 392. Goals 15. Honours: League Championship 64/65, 66/67; European Cup 67/68; FA Cup 62/63. 16 Scotland caps.

Made 39 appearances in the Championship season and is a well-known and respected radio analyst. An old-fashioned right-half in the true mould, he was bought from Celtic for £43,000 in 1963, and was one of the stars of that year's FA Cup victory.

He was variously described as being too slow, not a natural athlete, poor in the air and not a goal-scorer. Whatever the weaknesses were supposed to be, he overcame them all to be the heartbeat of the side. His long-distance passing became legendary and he seemed able to vary the pace of a game to suit the needs of the side. He was not a prolific scorer of goals but then he didn't need to be.

Paddy's connections with Manchester United endure. He had a brief spell as assistant under Tommy Docherty and can be seen at just about every home match passionately discussing the game. It was that passion and fervour that sometimes got him into trouble with referees and if there were problems on the field Paddy would never be far away. But he will always be best remembered for his enthusiasm and his devotion to the game and to the club.

He said: "The Championship going to United is not only a terrific boost for the club but for the English game in general. They are certainly capable of going on to win it all over again. I believe Alex Ferguson will now strengthen the side by bringing in a couple of players so that the club can make a serious challenge on the European Cup. For that reason, of course, he must look to bring in an English player or two if possible. The signing of Eric Cantona has been a very significant move on Fergie's part. He is a clever player and he is infectious. He has style and a touch of arrogance which suits the club's image.

"I wouldn't want to compare our side with this one because it is a different era, 26 years is a long time. Football is a very much faster and fiercer game now and you don't get as much time to dwell on the ball as in our day."

Bill Fowlkes

Born St Helens 5.1.32. Games 679. Goals 9. Honours: League Championship 55/56, 56/57, 64/65, 66/67; European Cup 67/68; FA Cup 62/63. 1 England cap.

Made 33 appearances in the Championship side. Works in promotions and public relations. A United man through and through, he was at the heart of the United defence in four Championship seasons and was at the veteran stage when they won it in 1967. Although often replaced by Ian Greaves in the 1955-56 season Bill never complained, but got on with his fanatical training so that when the call came he was always ready.

He played fullback in those days, and won his only England cap as a right-back against Ireland in a 2-0 win in October 1954, less than two years after making his United debut.

He was to play 17 seasons for United without another cap, though it was as a central defender in the wake of the Munich air crash that he was to find his best position. He was at his most magnificent when the battle was at its most physical. A powerfully-built man, exceptional in the air, he was only uncomfortable against the smaller, quicker strikers in the mould of Ian St John.

Perhaps one of the highlights of his long and distinguished career was the goal he scored against Real Madrid which put United into the European Cup final, for it enabled him to collect a European Cup medal at the age of 36. He stayed on at the club in various coaching positions before stepping out of football, but was there on the Championship night. At 61 he was grey haired, but still straight-backed and slim.

He said: "The team have shown they were better prepared to win it mentally than they were when they missed out in 1992. The development of Ince was an important factor because it meant they were able to play without Bryan Robson and not suffer from it. A lot of credit has gone to the forwards but as a defender I think it was the strongest United defence for four or five seasons. Peter Schmeichel was the best goalkeeper in Europe and the two central defenders, Pallister and Bruce, had a terrific season. They were an excellent pairing."

Nobby Stiles

Born Manchester 18.5.42. Games 392. Goals 19. Honours: League Championship 64/65, 66/67; European Cup 67/68. 28 England caps.

Made 37 appearances in the Championship side. Now the director of Manchester United's Centres of Excellence.

Nobby came through the club's junior ranks, but he became an international figure for his part in England's World Cup victory. The toothless Stiles grin became a trademark for the dogged little midfield player who had more to his game than an ability to snap and snarl at the ankles of opposing forwards. He was, of course, the archetypal aggressive player but he was also a great tactician who could sense danger and relieve it with a minimum of effort.

He could act as an effective defender alongside Foulkes and then fill the gap while Bobby Charlton went on those mazy runs from midfield which so electrified audiences not just at Old Trafford but wherever United or England played. Bobby was able to surge forward because he knew Nobby would be there to give cover. There was another side to his game, too, one that acted as an inspiration to his teammates. He was like Nigel Clough in the modern game. He was a polite, almost shy person off the pitch but on it he would issue the orders and lift the team when they needed lifting.

The story of his poor eyesight is well known, for it was after he was fitted with contact lenses that his timing improved. He left United and had a couple of seasons with Middlesbrough, eventually joining Preston North End where he became manager. He then joined his brother-in-law, Johnny Giles, at West Bromwich, becoming manager there before returning to his native Manchester to take up a post with the United set-up.

He said: "I love going to Old Trafford and watching the current side. They really excite and entertain. I love seeing a team attack with two wingers and one that has so much flair through the team. Since I came back to the club in 1989 I have been lucky to see them win something every season and I am confident that run will now continue for some years."

George Best

Born Belfast 22.5.46. Games 466. Goals 178. Honours: League Championship 64/65, 66/67; European Cup 67/68. 37 Northern Ireland caps.

Made 42 appearances in the Championship side. George now makes personal appearances, gives after-dinner speeches and acts as a television and radio analyst.

Without question George is one of the five greatest footballers the game has produced. But as with all sportsmen of genius there was a price to pay. It would be easy to suggest that his playing career never achieved total fulfilment, but that would be to detract from what he did offer his generation.

In his 11 seasons with United he left the supporters with the belief that they had witnessed a superstar to be compared only with Pele, Cruyff, Di Stefano and in more recent years Maradona. From his very first days at United it was clear that he was a special talent, a fitting idol for the times, playing football that was extraordinary in its imagination, skill and deadliness.

In 1968, with United champions, he had his best season. He was the top scorer in the First Division with 28 goals and the European and English Footballer of the Year. If his exploits off the pitch brought headlines bigger than those on it, then that was Best living the life to the full, though too often viewing it through the bottom of a bottle.

Sadly, we had seen the best of George. Once he left the club he appeared variously at Stockport, Fulham and Bournemouth with spells in between in the United States. He is, of course, still idolised by everyone with any feeling for United. He said: "This is a very fine team with a lot of class players in it. I have always admired talent that might win a match on its own and this side has those kind of players. Ryan Giggs is obviously one of those. I sit and watch him and it makes me feel I would like to be out there on the pitch with him. I can say that about very few players in the modern game."

Denis Law

Born Aberdeen 24.2.40. Games 393. Goals 236. Honours: League Championship 64/65, 66/67; FA Cup 62/63. 55 Scotland caps.

Made 36 appearances in the Championship side. Now a distinguished radio and TV analyst, an excellent anecdotal after-dinner speaker. He was brought to Old Trafford in 1962, after spells with Huddersfield Town under Bill Shankly, at Manchester City and then at Torino. The club paid the Italians £115,000 to bring him home, a British record at the time. He had come down from Aberdeen to Yorkshire as a tiny wisp of a boy and yet there was something about his impish presence, even as a teenager, that marked him down as the goal-poacher extraordinaire.

He had turned instinct into an art form by the time he came to Old Trafford, where the crowd nicknamed him the King. He didn't disappoint, crowning performance after performance with a phenomenal strike rate. In his first five seasons he was to score 160 goals in 222 matches, remarkable by any standards. Many of them were thrilling goals, too, and scored with justifiable arrogance. It is not difficult to picture him with his shirt outside his shorts and holding the cuffs of his shirt in the palms of his hands, signalling his goals with that one-armed salute that became so familiar to soccer fans.

His strengths were his uncanny ability to be where it mattered, almost as if he had read the move in advance; and that quick-as-lightning finish. He was to miss the European Cup run with knee trouble which dogged the rest of his career, though there are some United fans who never forgave Docherty for allowing him to move to Manchester City. But Denis is now a familiar figure at Old Trafford where his infectious humour can still pervade any gathering.

He said: "I think we have all waited so long for the title, all of us with a feeling for United. The signing of Eric Cantona was a master stroke on Fergie's part and it worked for him and the rest of the team perfectly. He has brought the best out in other players and given them confidence and he has been able to link up with Mark Hughes."

David Sadler

Born Yalding 5.2.46. Games 326. Goals 27. Honours: League Championship 66/67; European Cup 67/68. 4 England caps.

Made 34 appearances in the Championship winning side. Now organises corporate hospitality for Bobby Charlton Sports.

David Sadler is another member of the title winning side who took a back seas to the big names of Best, Law and Charlton and yet whose role in the overall marathon was a very important one. He was the antidote to the excitable Crerand, a gentleman with a quite unflappable nature who would remain cool whatever the provocation.

He had been a distinguished amateur player, representing England as a centre-forward at that level, and he brought the Corinthian spirit with him into the professional ranks where his attitude and sportsmanship were always exemplary.

After playing his first matches for the club as a centre-forward, he settled into a role in central defence where he was able to read the game and move forward when it was prudent to do so. He could distribute the ball with intelligence and these days, with footballing centre-halves in short supply, his type of game would have suited.

A valuable player who perhaps lacked the killer instinct, he was not destined to stay at Old Trafford, even though he had won four caps between 1967 and 1970. He moved on to Bolton in 1973, enjoying four happy seasons there and playing his best football. But David is still involved at United and is the man who keeps all the '67 side in touch with each other.

He said: "Most managers would be happy to have one world-class player in their side but we have had at least three this season and that has made all the difference to us winning the title. I don't think comparisons are easy and I would rather look ahead and think that this side now might dominate for a few seasons to come. Winning the title has lifted a burden from them and I think that will make things easier for them next season."

David Herd

Born Hamilton 15.5.34. Games 262. Goals 144. Honours: League Championship 64/65, 66/67; FA Cup 62/63. 5 Scotland caps.

Made 26 appearances in the Championship winning side, missing the final few games because of a broken leg. Now owns and runs a garage.

David always suffered from having to stand comparison with Denis Law, George Best and Bobby Charlton and was a more significant player at United than he has been given credit for over the years. But he played a key role in the success between '64 and '67, as his prolific strike rate demonstrates.

He did not, of course, have quite the equipment of those other forwards in terms of overall skill and ability to entertain. But what he did have was an ability to lead the line, which was crucial to the collective effort.

When Sir Matt brought him to Manchester he was already an international player and had scored a useful 97 goals in 166 performances for Arsenal. He slipped into the United side and was dependable without being spectacular. The arrival of Law from Italy lifted him in the way that Hughes has been lifted by the arrival of Cantona. He was perhaps at his most damaging when he had a run at goal, chasing those astute passes from Crerand. He was not noted as a powerful header, but he certainly could shoot.

The broken leg perhaps curtailed his career, for though he recovered and moved on to play a couple of seasons with Stoke City, he was never quite the same player again. He said: "I am just pleased that the ghost has been laid at last. I think this United has been developing for the last four seasons and this is when it has really come good. But remember they have won a trophy in each of those seasons. The United side I played in was consistent over five seasons and I believe this side can be the same. I hope they can go on to win the European Cup. I think that Cantona's arrival has made a big difference, especially to Hughes, who now has a partner to play alongside."

Bobby Charlton

Born Ashington 11.10.37. Games 752. Goals 247. Honours: League Championship 56/57, 64/65, 66/67; European Cup 67/68; FA Cup 62/63. 106 England caps.

Made 42 appearances in the Championship winning side. Now a director of Manchester United and of his own company, Bobby Charlton Sports, and several other enterprises.

The name of Bobby Charlton is revered wherever the game is played, attracting the same kind of adulation and respect as his old friend and adversary Pele. Bobby is like the original Boy's Own hero. He was the son of a miner who has always kept his own feet on the ground, a humble, honest man with a warmth of personality that is both captivating and contagious. As a player he had few betters, for to see Charlton with a ball at his feet was like watching a form of ballet. He had perfect co-ordination and wonderful explosions of pace, and his shooting was awesome. He was a player of great instinct and variety.

The Munich air tragedy affected Bobby deeply. He was a mere boy when they picked him from the slush on the runway, and he knew that he had to grow up immediately. Whether he played as a left winger, where he made his early appearances for England, or as a midfield player coming forward from deep positions, Charlton was a devastating finisher. It was in this position with Crerand alongside that he did perhaps most of his damage as a United star. He may not have favoured tackling and there were occasional lapses of concentration, but these are minor considerations weighed alongside his immense contribution to the national sport. He enjoyed a brief "cool down" to his career at Preston, where he also managed for a time.

But as an ambassador of his sport he is without equal. He said: "I think there are similarities between this side and the one with which we won the title. I think it is a blend of players which should serve our club well in the European Cup which obviously we would love to win. Like Alex's side now we had a very good goalkeeper, which is important and there is a lot of skill through the team, a lot of flair. But there is also some great resolve and toughness in players like Paul Ince."

Other players who took part in the winning of the 1967 Championship were:

John Aston

Born Manchester 28.6.47. Games 164. Goals 27. Honours: League Championship 66/67. European Cup 67/68. The son of former United idol John Aston, he played 26 matches and scored four goals in the season. A fast direct winger without frills.

Shay Brennan

Born Manchester 6.5.37. Games 355. Goals 6. Honours: League Championship 64/65, 66/67; European Cup 67/68. 19. Republic of Ireland caps. A shy, retiring man and a fine full-back with quick recovery, dependable rather than spectacular. Played 16 games. Came in after Noble's car crash.

John Connelly

Born St Helens 18.7.38. Games 112. Goals 35. Honours: League Championship 64/65. 20 England caps. A member of the World Cup winning squad of 1966, Connelly played seven matches in the Championship side and scored twice. A winger in the old-fashioned mould.

David Gaskell

Born Wigan 5.10.40. Games 118. Goals 0. Honours: FA Cup 63/64. Played five times as occasional stand-in when Alex Stepney was injured. Made his debut as a 16-year-old sub for Ray Wood in the Charity Shield at Maine Road in 1956.

Noel Cantwell

Born Cork 28.2.32. Games 144. Goals 8. Honours: FA Cup 62/63. 36 Republic of Ireland caps. A dominating figure, he took over the centre-half role in the '67 side on four occasions, though he had skippered the team that lifted the FA Cup in '63.

Jimmy Ryan

Born Stirling 12.5.45. Games 24. Goals 4. Honours: None. Never did justice to his ability at Old Trafford but was drafted in on four occasions to fill in for injury in the title season.

Harry Gregg

Born Derry 25.10.32. Games 247. Goals 0. Honours: 25 Northern Ireland caps. Perhaps the best goalkeeper United ever had, yet with no club honours to show for it. Made two appearances in the Championship season.

John Fitzpatrick

Born Aberdeen 18.8.46. Games 141. Goals 10. Honours: None. Made three appearances in the season when he was considered to be the understudy to Nobby Stiles.

Willie Anderson

Born Liverpool 24.1.47. Games 10. Goals 0. Honours: None. Made just one appearance throughout the season. Willie was not destined to stay long at Old Trafford, moving on to enjoy the bulk of his career at Aston Villa and then Cardiff.

The Next 26 Years

What about the next 26 years? According to Alex Ferguson's managerial colleagues across the nation he has it cracked. Some see a river of success flowing out from Old Trafford, engulfing not only the best in England but the Continent too. "Can you become the AC Milan of English football?" an Italian journalist demanded of Ferguson an hour after United's big Championship celebration match against Blackburn on May 3rd.

The question was sincere. United are English football's true world power. Visitors from across the globe had attended the party. Ferguson smiled and turned to Martin Edwards, by his side on the Press room rostrum. "First I have to ask our chairman if he has as much money as Silvio Berlusconi," he told the man from Milan, referring to the owner of Italy's most powerful club. "But I have to say it's much harder for English clubs to dominate like AC have done. We must recognise the strength of our league compared with elsewhere in Europe."

Ferguson might have added that, apart from competing with the mountain of lira TV magnate Berlusconi pours into his San Siro operation, there is the small matter of competing with Jack Walker's Blackburn 28 miles up the road. Uncle Jack, as he is known to Ewood Park manager Kenny Dalglish, could tip the balance of football power in Britain. There has never been a football handout like the £30 million interest-free loan to Rovers from the £350 million sale by Walker and his brother of the family steel business.

Neither the Edwards family at Old Trafford, nor even the Moores dynasty at Everton, have been prepared to bankroll a football dream to that extent. At the same time it doesn't need a crystal ball to see that United are a blue chip investment. As one club chairman remarked, with more than a tinge of jealousy, to the club's commercial manager Danny McGregor: "The place is a licence to print money."

Every time someone sticks a fork into a chop at one of Old Trafford's restaurants the football club benefits. Each time a boy asks his dad for a United outfit for his birthday or buys a scarf at the souvenir shop United's finances are boosted. International companies vie for the privilege of having their name on United's shirt or supplying replica United kits.

How many clubs in the world can seat 2,000 diners at matches? United can. What other English ground has 147 executive boxes costing anything up to £18,750 per campaign and a lengthy queue waiting to take the next that becomes available? It all comes down to the best commercial operation in British football and it earns United a cool £10 million profit a year – roughly as much cash as that generated by the football.

Nothing, of course, would work if there wasn't success on the field. The training ground and dressing room are the natural springs from where the football cash begins to flow. Here there is real quality. It could easily put the club in pole position of the league game for a decade. Yet Ferguson was wise to play the taciturn Scot even as he raised the new Premier League pot into the Old Trafford skies. He counselled everyone that hunger for success was the vehicle's main drive. Without it, he reminded his young side, the wheels would drop off. There would be much jaw work from him to ensure it didn't happen and a lot of research too.

Ferguson is a workaholic who has been compared in his management style to Matt Busby. The comparison errs. Matt was an uncle to his players. Ferguson is a dominating, even bullying father. There is much more of the caution and mental toughness of Don Revie in him than the avuncular Matt. No manager prepares his side better. None consumes more travelling hours to ensure they know all about their opponents down to the length of their toenails. Nothing is left to chance. There is no rest for such men. Ferguson might ultimately seize up but the inner drive will not. In his own words: "It is my intention to keep the pedal down. It's not in my nature to do otherwise."

There is little doubt that Ferguson, who was 51 when he lifted the title, will spend the rest of his working life at Old Trafford. His contract, worth around £200,000, is due to expire when he was 55. It could be extended, though it is highly unlikely he would want to emulate Busby and still be in active management beyond his 60th birthday. It is more likely he would become a club director or even general manager with a younger man doing the ramrod role with the team. Such a man could only pursue the very best and at a cost of some £19 million Ferguson has rebuilt the spine of United's side from goalkeeper through midfield to attack.

His title team had an international player in every position but one – that occupied by team captain and centre back Steve Bruce. Most were young enough to be considered in their prime for another five years. In any case there were a dozen brilliant 18-year-olds waiting for their chance to step on to Old Trafford's big stage.

This was the area where Ferguson had to tread a tightrope. He was the first United manager since Busby to develop the grassroots of the club.

He regarded it as a quest, this return to a policy that garnered the best young talent in the game at Old Trafford in the Fifties. You don't do that and then let your young shoots be trampled underfoot – and that is why the United manager was determined to tread carefully in the transfer market.

Ferguson, indeed, hardly needed to go on a recruiting drive. There was already an emerging crop of stars who were jostling for elbow room in the United dressing room through to the next century. Fergie's Fledglings were perhaps not emerging with the force of the Busby Babes who won the FA Youth Cup five years in succession from 1953 to 1957.

That group went on to provide a United side that in 1956 took the First Division title, finishing 11 points ahead of second-placed Blackpool, with an average age of 22. No-one at Old Trafford was making comparison with that Colossus of a wing half, Duncan Edwards, forwards like Tommy Taylor and Dennis Viollet or defenders of the calibre of Roger Byrne and Mark Jones. But Ferguson's group looked the closest any United manager had assembled. They had contested two FA Youth Cup summits in successive seasons.

The jewel in United's youth operation was, of course, Ryan Giggs. He was the first Old Trafford youngster who could be compared without rose-tinting to the embryonic George Best. Giggs's performances, which Italian eyes were watching with interest, rocketed his transfer value to £10 million.

There is a nice Giggs story that captures exactly Ferguson's dog-at-a-bone style when it comes to recruiting young stars. Manchester City had been tipped off about the potential of the 13-year-old Salford schools player. But the man who turned up on young Giggs' doorstep on his 14th birthday was Ferguson. Before the lad knew what had hit him he had signed associate schoolboy forms and the greatest talent to emerge in Manchester in a generation was under wraps. There were other new kids on the block whose talent was blossoming with Eric Harrison, the youth team manager.

Keith Gillespie, a young right winger from Best country – Larne in Northern Ireland – scored on his first team debut against Bury in the FA Cup. He has a natural eye for a goal and great crossing ability.

Central defenders Gary Neville and Chris Casper were described as being like peas in a pod by United's training staff. Neville, tall and skilful, comes from Bury and first appeared briefly in United's UEFA Cup game against Torpedo Moscow at Old Trafford in September 1992. Casper is the teenage son of former Burnley striker and manager Frank Casper and – as with seniors Pallister and Bruce – dovetails easily with his partner. David Beckham is a creative, elegant midfielder from London who made his first-team debut in the last 20 minutes at Brighton in the Coca Cola Cup, also in September '92.

Mancunian Nicky Butt combines a good touch in midfield with good tackling ability. He came on as a first-team substitute against Oldham in November '92. They like wingers at Old Trafford and the youth side has one who could put the pressure on Giggs and Lee Sharpe in young Ben Thornley. He has pace and two good feet, though he prefers to raid down the left. These were the pick of Old Trafford's trainees at the time the Premier League trophy was being tucked away in United's cabinet, and Ferguson intended to give his entire group of 18 youngsters full professional contracts.

"They are the best crop I've had in my management career. A lot of people tell me they could even be the best the club has ever had," he said. "To have such quality come through at the same time is very rare. Now it's just a matter of fitting them into the first team when the opportunity arises." Ferguson is a man who nurtures his young blooms. The United manager remembers with anguish how overexposure withered a particularly promising group he had when he managed Aberdeen. What could have been an assembly of talent to buttress Pittodrie for a decade was burned out through premature use in a couple of years. Since then Ferguson's guiding principle with young players has been: Don't go to the well too often.

It was undoubtedly irksome to the hordes of journalists who converged on Old Trafford as the Championship reached a gripping climax that the club's best young talent, Ryan Giggs, did not voice a word about himself or his work.

It seemed a contradiction that a teenage boy could be asked to perform like a man on that huge and frightening stage but not away from it. Only when the Championship was in the bag and Giggs had decorated the Old Trafford celebrations with a marvellous goal against Blackburn were the wraps taken off. Ryan Giggs spoke!

Ferguson's natural caution was understandable. He remembered that a generation ago Best was a shy, reticent teenager before all the world wanted a piece of his genius. The United manager had no intention of letting the locusts settle on his playing field. For the next ten years, or perhaps even twenty, he was planning to make Old Trafford a Field of Dreams.

Acknowledgements

The authors would like to thank Daily Express Sports Editor David
Emery, Geoff Critchley, David Fletcher and the Daily Express Sports
team without whom this book could not have been produced.
Also SLG Business Services for their enthusiasm and hard work,
Keene Engraving and The Bath Press for their support.

Devised and Edited by Frank Malley
Additional editing by Peter Boyle, Andrew Elliott and Chris Gill
Picture research by Mick Lidbury